Secure Your WordPress Website with HTTPS for free

A Visual Step-by-Step Guide to Securing Your Website with SSL

Updated 4th April 2018

Dr. Andy Williams

https://ezseonews.com

"I work in the education department at one of the top academic institutions in the U.S. and if I could hire Dr. Williams to write all of my online training, I wouldn't hesitate..." ***Laurie***

DISCLAIMER AND TERMS OF USE AGREEMENT

The author and publisher of this eBook and the accompanying materials have used their best efforts in preparing this eBook. The author and publisher make no representation or warranties with respect to the accuracy, applicability, fitness, or completeness of the contents of this eBook. The information contained in this eBook is strictly for educational purposes. Therefore, if you wish to apply ideas contained in this eBook, you are taking full responsibility for your actions.

The author and publisher disclaim any warranties (express or implied), merchantability, or fitness for any particular purpose. The author and publisher shall in no event be held liable to any party for any direct, indirect, punitive, special, incidental or other consequential damages arising directly or indirectly from any use of this material, which is provided "as is", and without warranties.

The author and publisher do not warrant the performance, effectiveness or applicability of any sites listed or linked to in this eBook.

All links are for information purposes only and are not warranted for content, accuracy or any other implied or explicit purpose.

The author and publisher of this book are not in any way associated with Google.

Contents

How to Use this Book

I do not recommend you just sit down and read this book. The problem is that a lot of this book describes processes that you actually need to do on your computer. If you try to read without following along on your computer you'll get lost and not know what I am talking about.

This book is a hands-on tutorial. I recommend that you sit at your computer with the book open in front of you to get the most out of it. You can then just follow along and work your way through the process. Whenever I do something, you do it too.

By the end of this book, you'll be comfortable converting HTTP WordPress websites to secure HTTPS sites.

Prefer a video course?

Some people prefer to read a book while others want something to view. I have a video course on this topic for those who want to watch the entire process over my shoulder—so to speak. The video course closely follows the format of this book.

You can get the video course at a huge discount through this link:

https://ezseonews.com/httpscourse

A note about UK vs US English

There are some differences between UK and US English. While I try to be consistent, errors may sometimes slip into my writing. This is because I spend a lot of time corresponding with people in both the UK and the US. The lines can blur.

Examples of this include spelling of words like optimise (UK) vs optimize (US).

The difference I get the most complaints about is with collective nouns. Collective nouns refer to a group of individuals, e.g. Google. In the US, collective nouns are singular, so **Google IS** a search engine. In the UK, though, collective nouns are usually plural, so **Google ARE** a search engine.

There are other differences too. If I've been inconsistent anywhere in this book I hope that it doesn't detract from the value you get from it.

Found Typos in this book?

Occasional errors can get through proofreaders too. I'd be very grateful if you could let me know if you find any typos or grammatical mistakes in this book. You can report those using this email address:

typos@ezseonews.com

Please include the title of the book in any email. Thanks!

Which Web Host?

You may already have your web hosting sorted out. If you do, then please make sure it meets the requirements of this book. It's quite simple.

You need a cPanel host that supports server name indication (SNI).

What if your server doesn't support SNI? In this case, you'll need each domain you want to protect located on its own unique IP address. The only reason you would need this is if you want to support older clients. Windows XP (Microsoft support for XP ended on 8 April 2014) running Internet Explorer is an example. All the modern operating systems and web browsers today support SNI.

If you're not sure then ask your host. If it doesn't support SNI, you won't be able to implement Full (Strict) SSL without buying a dedicated IP address. You will, however, still be able to use Flexible SSL.

If you don't already have web hosting I highly recommend you use Stablehost for the reasons below:

- I've been using Stablehost for several years. It's the best "budget" web host I've ever used in terms of support and features.
- The screenshots in this book are from within the cPanel of Stablehost. This makes it easier to follow everything you see.
- I have a 40% discount code you can use when you sign up. You get 40% off your first payment whether that's for one month or three years.
- It's cPanel hosting which is what I use to illustrate in this book.
- It offers AutoSSL and Encrypt It! Integration for free.
- Supports SNI, so you can use Full (Strict) SSL (more on that later).

You can read my article here if you want to take full advantage of the 40% discount with Stablehost:

https://ezseonews.com/whysh

That article is my review of Stablehost and explains why I use them. The same web page also includes the 40% discount code.

I recommend Namecheap as a registrar. It is free to sign up. The article below shows how to use Namecheap as a registrar and link it to Stablehost web hosting:

https://ezseonews.com/host

The article provides step-by-step instructions.

What you will learn in this book

This book will take you through the process of upgrading your site from HTTP to HTTPS. Here's what we're going to cover:

- What is SSL and should you switch?
- How HTTPS works.
- What is AutoSSL and what you can do if your web host supports it?
- Check if you already have an HTTPS version of your site.
- Why having an HTTP and HTTPS version of your site at the same time can be a problem.
- Cloudflare - what is it, why I use it, and why you should use it too?
- Add a website to Cloudflare and update your domain registrar so that your site runs through it.
- The types of SSL offered by Cloudflare.
- The differences between Flexible SSL, Full SSL, and Full (strict) SSL.
- Origin and Edge certificates.
- Generate & Install an SSL certificate.
- Remove old certificates.
- Understand and fix mixed content.
- Secure your WordPress Dashboard and what to do if you get locked out.
- Redirect the HTTP pages to HTTPS pages.
- Test your SSL and fix problems.
- Update or change your existing SSL certificate for another one.

What is SSL and why switch?

SSL stands for **Secure Socket Layer**.

SSL is a security technology. It establishes an encrypted connection between a web server (website) and a browser. All data that moves between the server and the web browser is encrypted. That means data stays private even if someone intercepts the information. For a server to be secure it needs an SSL certificate.

NOTE: You may also hear people talking about TLS. TLS stands for **Transport Layer Security.** It's a new stronger encryption protocol that does the same basic thing. You'll often hear SSL and TLS used interchangeably though it's not actually correct.

How does this work?

When the browser connects to the server it requests the server identity.

The server identifies itself by sending the SSL certificate, including the server's public key.

After creating a secure connection to a web page the session key encrypts all data transmitted between visitors and the web server. This is vital, especially when transmitting sensitive data to or from a web browser.

For example, when you buy something online you enter data a thief could exploit to use with your credit card. That information MUST remain private. To ensure it does, SSL (or TLS) encrypts all information moving back and forth. Modern web browsers show a green padlock with the word Secure. This shows visitors the website has this type of security and is safe to use.

Web Content Studio 20
Secure
https://webcontentstudio.com

You will also notice that the web address of the web page begins with **HTTPs.**

This site has an SSL certificate and is secure. Any information transmitted between the website and the web browser of a visitor (or client) is secure and private. The information is encrypted.

Not secure
andyjwilliams.co.uk

So what about unsecured websites? Well, Google Chrome now shows a red triangle with an exclamation mark inside it and the words **Not secure** at the side. This site is NOT using an SSL certificate. That means all information passed between the visitor and website is in plain text format. It's therefore easy for any savvy thief to intercept and read that stream of data.

Why use SSL?

There are many reasons why everyone should use SSL to secure their website. Some of these only apply to sites that collect sensitive information. Other reasons apply to ALL websites.

Here are the reasons that apply to “normal” sites that don’t collect sensitive data:

1. Visitor confidence

The example above is the first reason you should be using an SSL certificate. What does a **Not Secure** message tell your visitors? With cybercrime on the rise and constantly in the news no one wants to visit insecure websites.

A document [1] published by GlobalSign (GMO Internet Group) stated that 75% of web users are aware of security risks. Another 77% have concerns about someone intercepting their data. The document stated that 9 out of 10 users are more likely to buy something when they know it’s from a secure connection.

2. Browsers are pushing for it

Google Chrome was one of the first to start penalizing insecure sites with messages. Other browsers have since followed suit. In fact, in 2015, Mozilla (Firefox) announced they intend to “phase out non-secure HTTP”. That essentially meant ending support for insecure websites.

At the time of writing, Google Chrome only shows the insecure message on web pages that request sensitive information. However, it plans to roll this out to ALL websites irrespective of whether they actually collect any information or not.

3. HTTPS is a Google ranking factor

It’s not a very strong one at the moment. If two web pages are identical in terms of “ranking power”, with nothing else to differentiate them, Google will rank the secure web page above the unsecured one.

Then we have the reasons that apply to sites that DO collect sensitive data:

1. SSL encrypts sensitive data

This is the main reason we want to use SSL on our website. It's particularly important when a web page asks for sensitive information. This includes things like usernames, passwords, credit card details, and so on. When a server is secure, any information you enter into a web form is only readable by the server you send it to. The server is the only computer that has the “code” to make sense of the encrypted data.

2. SSL authenticates a website

Authentication essentially means an SSL certificate guarantees safe data transfer. You can be sure the data you send goes to the right server and not to a thief pretending to be that server.

3. SSL is essential for Payment Card Industry (PCI) compliance

If you want to accept credit card payments your processor will need a properly installed

SSL certificate on your site.
One of the biggest disadvantages of SSL is the cost. SSL certificates often come with a hefty monthly or annual fee. However, this book will show you free options. Note that I would not use free options if I accepted credit cards on my site or ran a large eCommerce business. The free options are fine for the average site that wants to take advantage of the security and visitor confidence it instills.

References

1. http://downloads.globalsign.com/acton/attachment/2674/f-0360/1/-/-/-/-/increase-conversions-with-SSL.pdf

How HTTPS works

The “S” in HTTPs stands for security (secure). Http is insecure.

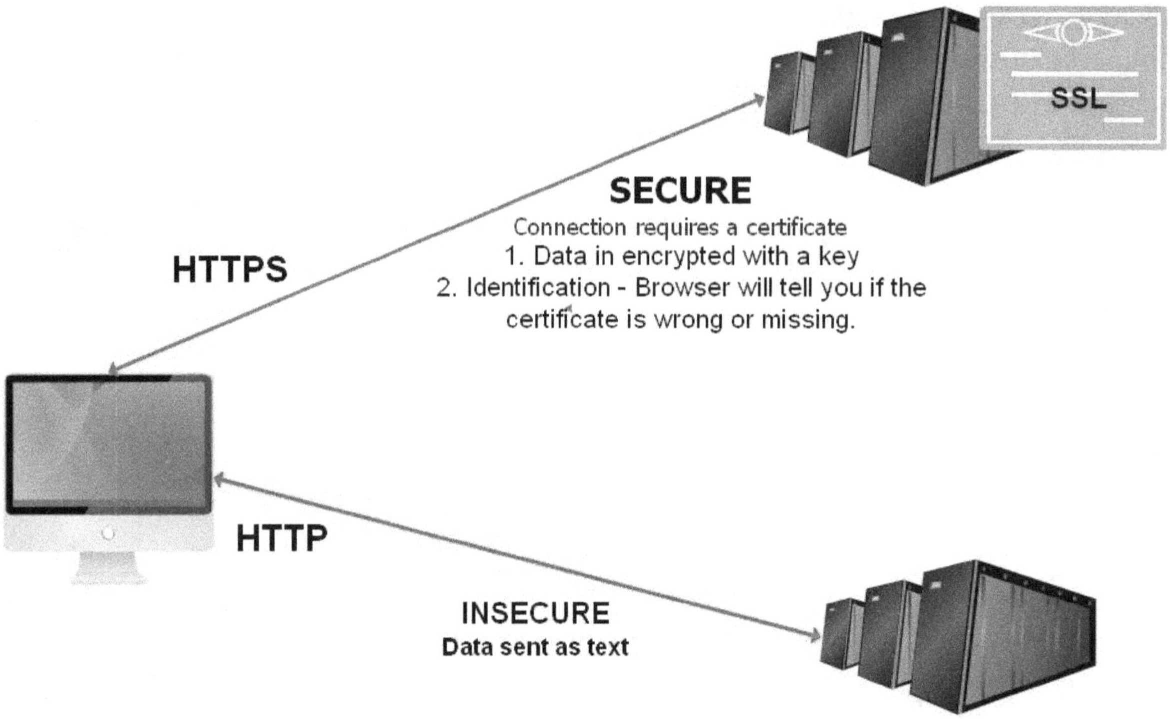
SSL
SECURE
Connection requires a certificate
1. Data in encrypted with a key
2. Identification - Browser will tell you if the certificate is wrong or missing.
HTTPS
HTTP
INSECURE
Data sent as text

When you access a website it sends data from one computer to another. It's possible for a hacker to intercept that data. When you interact with an HTTP website the information sent is in plain “English” (or another language). That means cybercriminals can read it easily.

All information is encrypted when you connect to an HTTPs site. That means any stolen data is useless to a thief. This is the kind of security people demand when they use credit cards online.

Your site needs a certificate issued by a certificate authority for this security to work. The certificate is then stored on your web server. When someone accesses your website their browser looks for the certificate. It's then checked against the authority that issued it. As long as everything checks out, the browser can then display the web page.

If there's a problem with the certificate there will be a warning message that looks something like this:

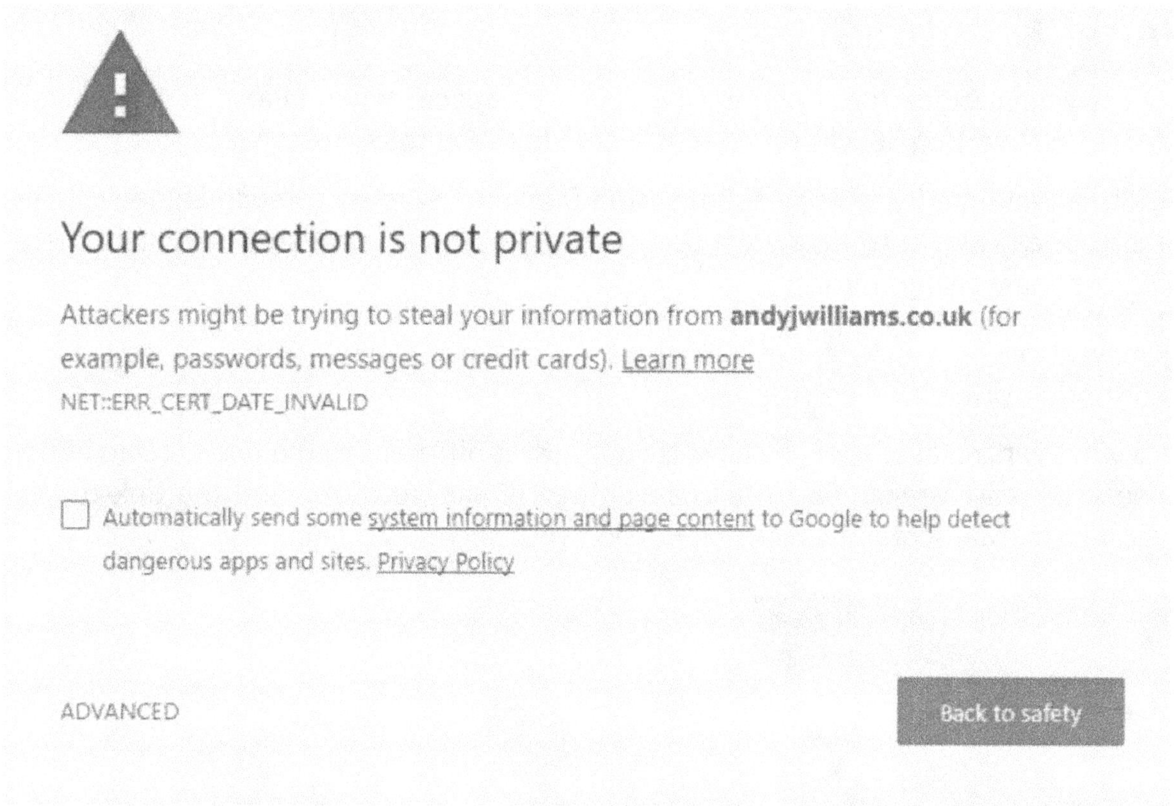
Your connection is not private
Attackers might be trying to steal your information from andyjwilliams.co.uk (for example, passwords, messages or credit cards). Learn more
NET::ERR_CERT_DATE_INVALID
Automatically send some system information and page content to Google to help detect dangerous apps and sites. Privacy Policy
ADVANCED
Back to safety

That was a warning message I got trying to access one of my own websites. There was no current certificate for the site so when the browser went looking for it, it reported the problem.

"Your connection is not private"

Simply translated, "there isn't a valid certificate for this site".

cPanel & AutoSSL

cPanel is your toolbox for administering your web space. When cPanel & WHM (Web Host Manager) version 58 was released it included the AutoSSL feature.

AutoSSL can automatically request and install Domain Validated Comodo-Signed SSL for your site. It can also auto-renew the certificate. This is free to cPanel admins so there shouldn't be any charge for it.

You may also see a link to **Let's Encrypt** inside your cPanel. This is a certificate authority that offers free certificates.

Check what version of cPanel you have if your host is different to the one I recommend. You need at least version 58 to take advantage of the AutoSSL. Find the link to the Server Information screen to see what version your server is running:

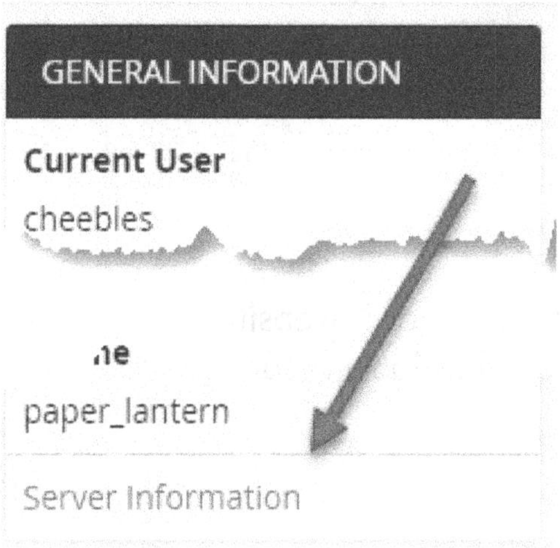
GENERAL INFORMATION
Current User
cheebles
paper_lantern
Server Information

Click on **Server Information** to see the details:

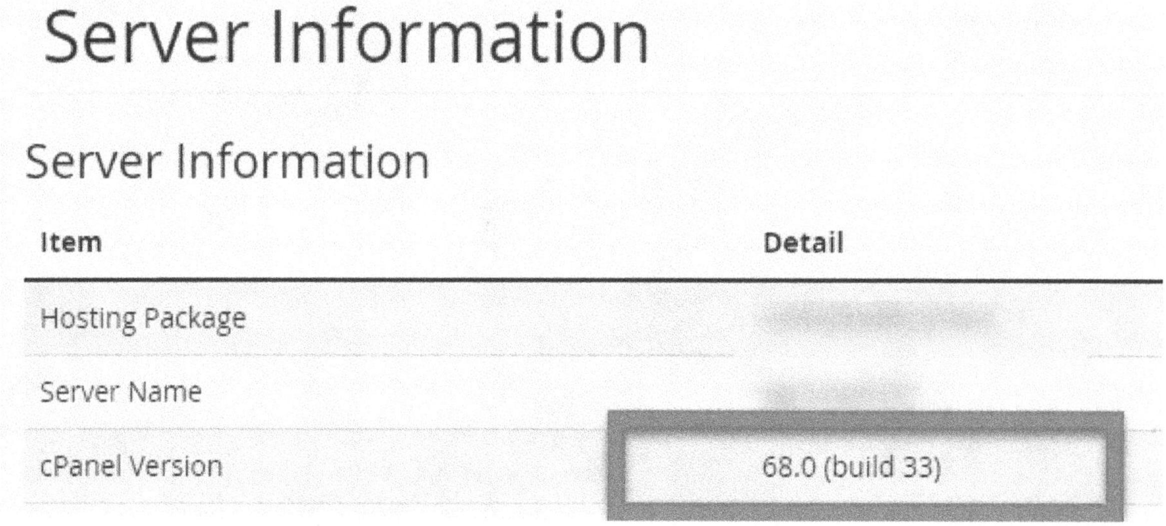
Server Information
Server Information
Item
Detail
Hosting Package
Server Name
cPanel Version
68.0 (build 33)

Check if HTTPS is already present

OK, we've looked at cPanel and AutoSSL and how AutoSSL automatically creates a secure version of your website. You'll have AutoSSL enabled by default if you use my recommended web host.

Simply type in your domain name with HTTPs instead of HTTP to see if your website has a secure version. Here is the HTTP version of a test site of mine:

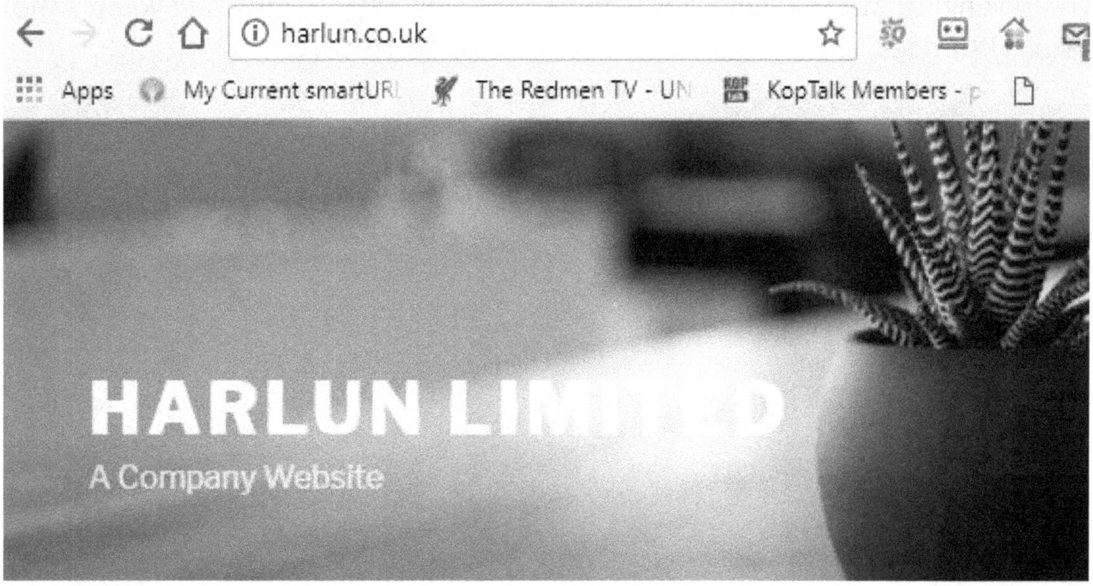
harlun.co.uk
Apps
My Current smartURL
The Redmen TV - UN
KopTalk Members - p
HARLUN LIMITED
A Company Website

The insecure HTTP version loads just fine.

If I try the HTTPs version, I get this:

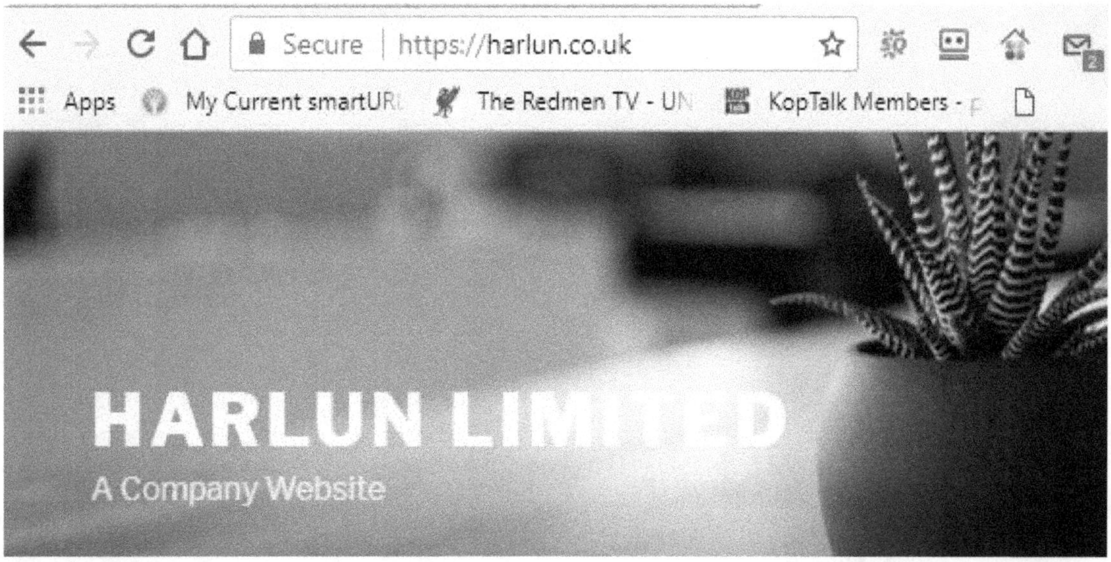
Secure
https://harlun.co.uk
Apps
My Current smartURL
The Redmen TV - UN
KopTalk Members - p
HARLUN LIMITED
A Company Website

The HTTPs version is also working fine. That is because AutoSSL automatically created a certificate for this site—and it works!

You may not get the padlock and "Secure" message when you try. This is because of something called **mixed content**. Here's what you could see instead:

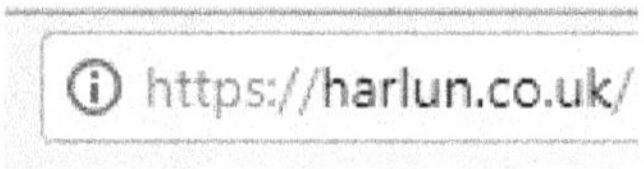
https://harlun.co.uk/

In place of the padlock and secure message you get a circle with "i" inside.

We will look at that later in the book and see how to fix this mixed (or insecure) content. What you're looking for at the moment is whether the web page loads when you try the HTTPs version. If it does, then you at least have a valid certificate.

HTTP AND HTTPS is not a good idea

Earlier in the book I showed you these two URLs:

http://harlun.co.uk

https://harlun.co.uk

Both URLs worked, and both loaded the exact same web page. But did you know that Google treats these as two separate web pages!

Links to your site will help with your search engine rankings. However, a link to one or other of these two URLs only helps that one version of the web page, not both. And if someone wants to link to your site, which URL do you tell them to use?

The answer is to redirect all requests for the HTTP version of the page to the HTTPs version. This way, only one version will be available and it will be the secure version.

This book will show you how to redirect all HTTP versions of the URL to the HTTPS version. This should also divert any link juice from outside sites so that all links point at the single, valid, HTTPS version of the URL.

Why Cloudflare

I've been using Cloudflare for years as a content delivery network (CDN). A CDN is essentially a network of computers that contain copies of your website. When someone visits your site they receive a copy that's closest to them geographically. If that copy is unavailable, for any reason, the CDN delivers the next closest copy. Using a CDN not only makes your web pages load faster, it can also mean your site's up 100% of the time!

Here's a graph that shows a website I ran on a web host (Hostgator) without Cloudflare:

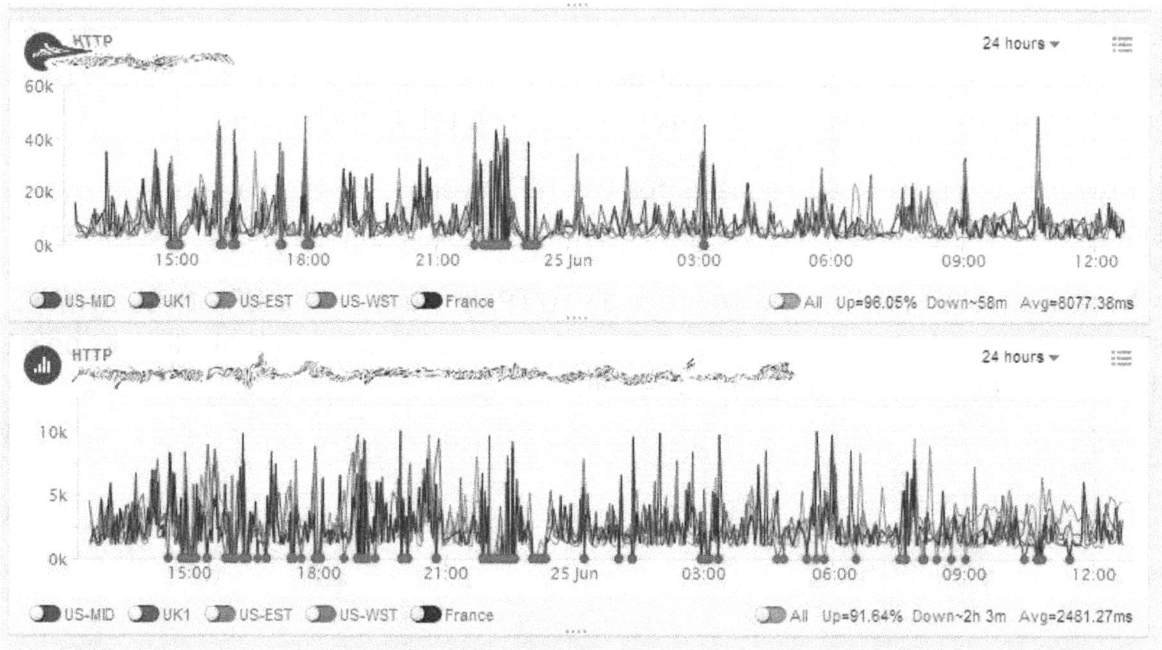

HTTP
24 hours
60k
40k
20k
0k
15:00
18:00
21:00
25 Jun
03:00
06:00
09:00
12:00
US-MID
UK1
US-EST
US-WST
France
All Up=96.05% Down~58m Avg=8077.38ms
HTTP
24 hours
10k
5k
0k
15:00
18:00
21:00
25 Jun
03:00
06:00
09:00
12:00
US-MID
UK1
US-EST
US-WST
France
All Up=91.64% Down~2h 3m Avg=2481.27ms

The top graph is the homepage and the lower graph is an internal page on the site.

The homepage was down and unavailable for 58 minutes in that 24 hour period. And the server took nearly 8 seconds to respond when a visitor came to my site. That's 8 seconds BEFORE it started to load my web page and NOT 8 seconds to load the actual page!

The internal page was down for over two hours in that 24-hour period.

I actually moved that site away from Hostgator to Stablehost. That was when I implemented Cloudflare on the site.

Here's the graph that shows the site migrating across to the Stablehost server (the left half of the image). You can also see the moment I switched on Cloudflare (red arrow):

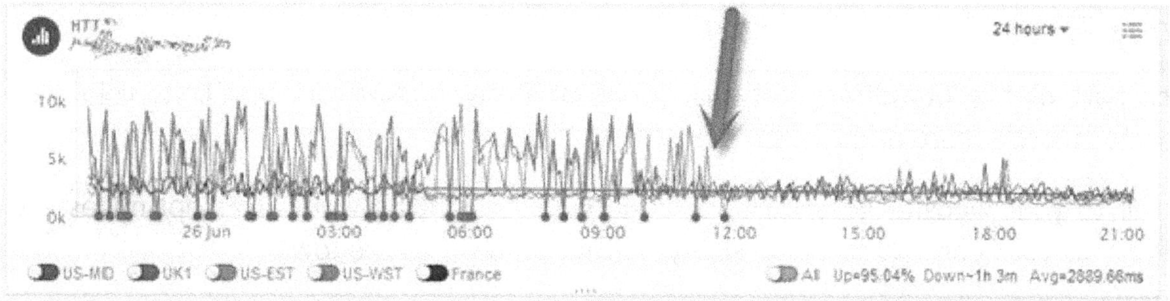
24 hours
10k
5k
0k
26 Jun
03:00
06:00
09:00
12:00
15:00
18:00
21:00
US-MD
UK1
US-EST
US-WST
France
All Up=95.04% Down=1h 3m Avg=2889.66ms

We cannot draw too many conclusions from that graph though. The site was moving from Hostgator to Stablehost and Cloudflare was just starting to kick in. After the site fully migrated and was using Cloudflare the graph looked like this:

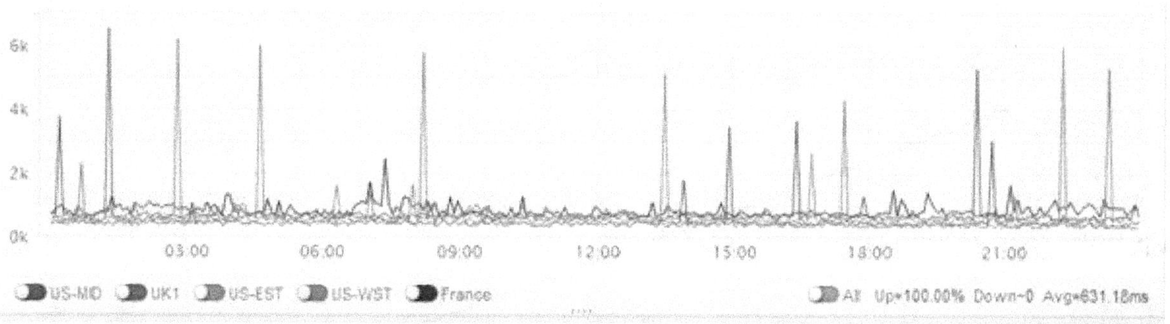
6k
4k
2k
0k
03:00
06:00
09:00
12:00
15:00
18:00
21:00
US-MD
UK1
US-EST
US-WST
France
All Up=100.00% Down=0 Avg=631.18ms

In the previous 24 hours, the site was up 100% of the time. Look at the server response time too. It went right down to 0.6 seconds!

If those were not reason enough to use Cloudflare, let me go one step further in convincing you.

It's free!

Many web hosts integrate Cloudflare, including the one I recommend in this book.

Cloudflare can also secure your website by acting as a proxy between your visitors and website server. It's effective at filtering out malicious visitors before they can wreak havoc on the server or waste your valuable bandwidth.

I recommend Cloudflare for four reasons ...

1. Protection
2. Save Bandwidth
3. Faster Page Loading and less downtime
4. It's free

How Cloudflare works

Once part of the Cloudflare network (Content Delivery Network or CDN), your site becomes more secure and loads faster.

Traffic to your website goes through Cloudflare's global network. This optimizes the delivery of your content to every visitor so that load times are low.

Cloudflare will also block threats and limit abusive bots & crawlers. This feature protects your site and prevents wasted bandwidth and server resources.

I'll explain what this all means using diagrams.

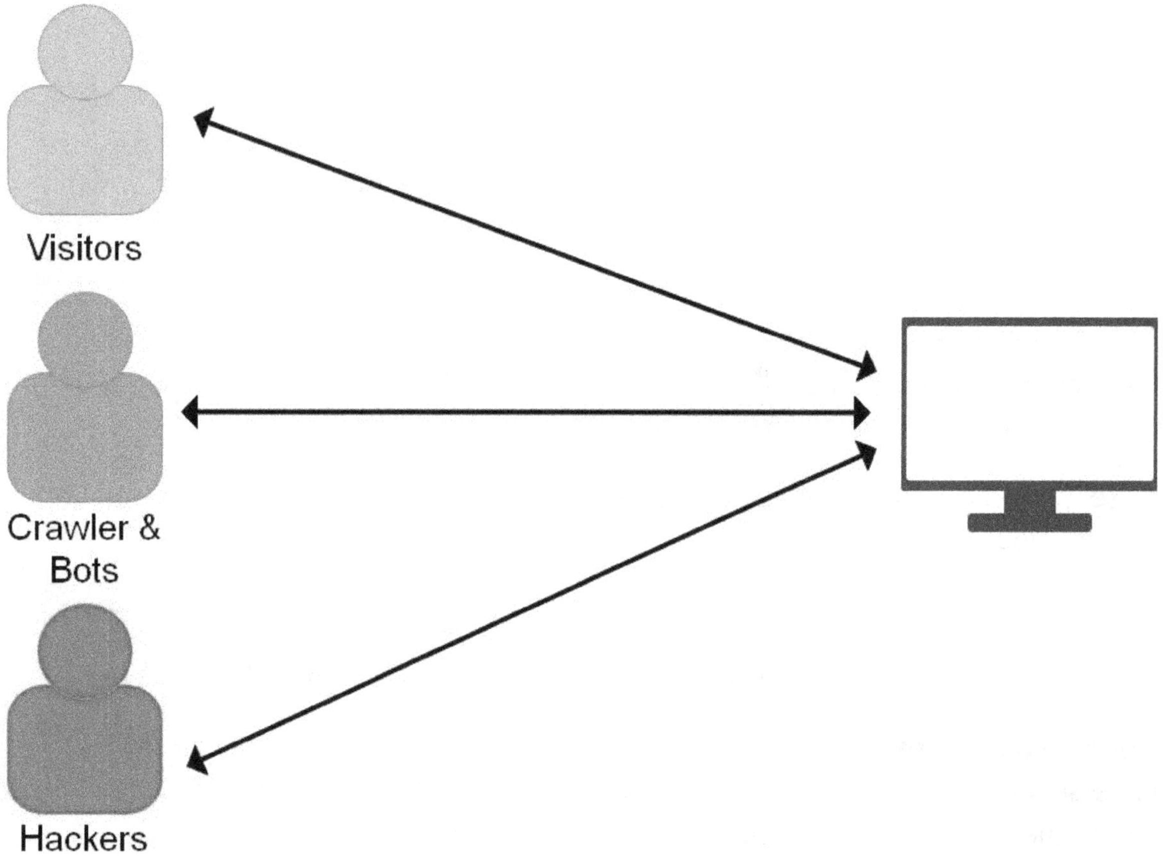
Visitors
Crawler & Bots
Hackers

We have three main types of traffic coming to our website.

- Visitors - we want to encourage this type of traffic to come, interact, share posts, and return to the site.
- Crawlers & Bots - This group of traffic is a mixed bag. We want certain crawlers and bots to come to the site, e.g. Google Bot, which spiders the site and takes back important information about our content to the search engine. However, there are also malicious bots and crawlers out there for no good purpose. These

are definitely not something we should encourage.

- Hackers – Obviously this is another malicious group we do not want on our website.

On a website without Cloudflare, there's no filter to protect it from malicious visitors. All three groups of visitors shown in that diagram have free access to do as they please.

When you add Cloudflare to your site, you're adding in the power of the global network and everything it's learned. Cloudflare acts as a good first line of defense for filtering traffic:

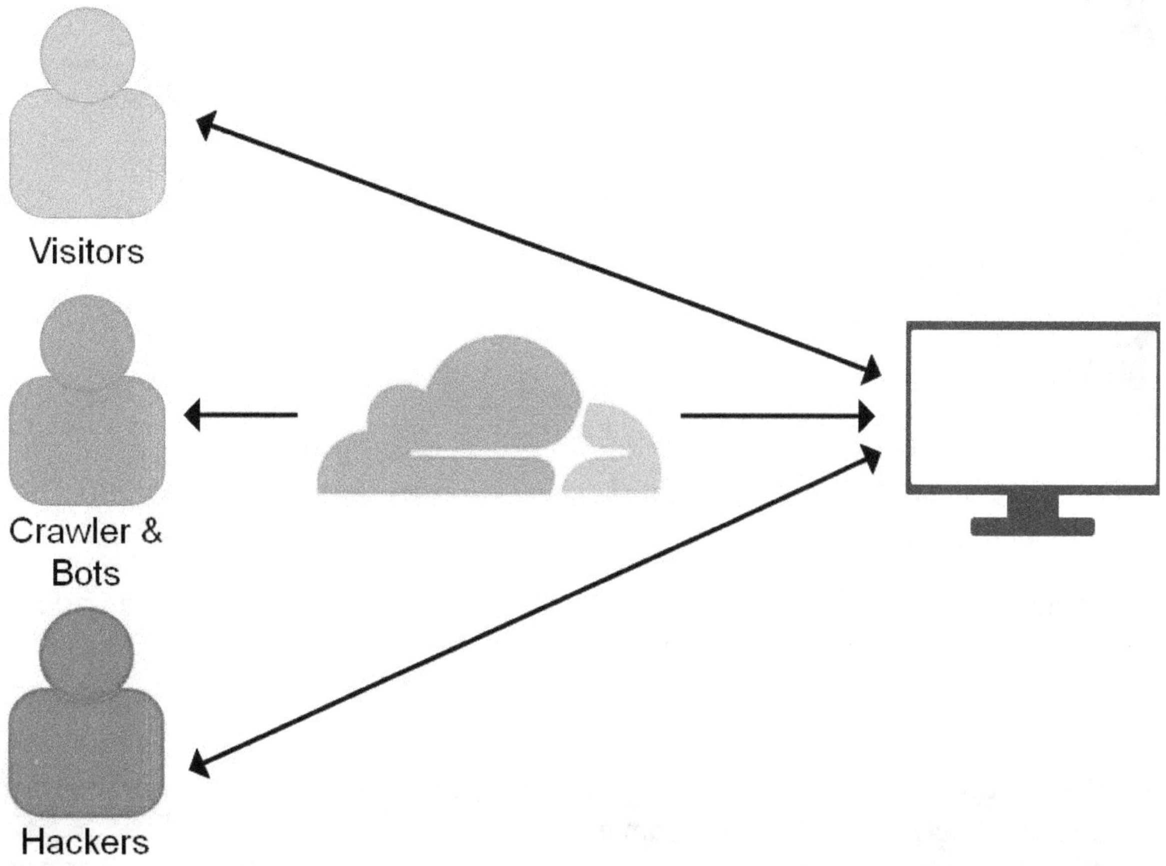
Visitors
Crawler & Bots
Hackers

The Cloudflare network filters the crawlers and bots so that only those you want to get through actually do. This is a community "project". As people add more sites to the network, the more threats it detects and learns to deal with. In essence, Cloudflare gets more intelligent over time.

Cloudflare is even more efficient against hackers:

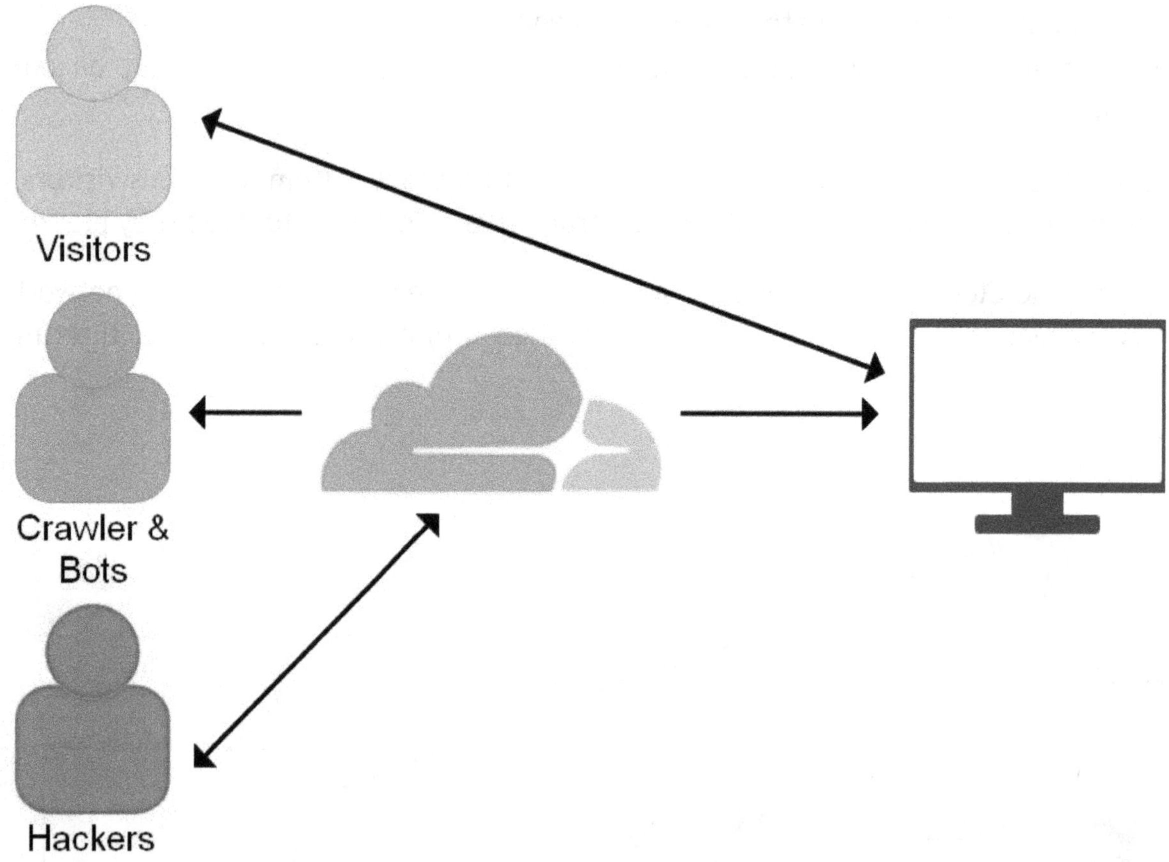
Visitors
Crawler &
Bots
Hackers

Cloudflare filters out the traffic from hackers as it passes through the network. That means they don't even reach your website in the first place.

This filtering feature of Cloudflare has nothing to do with HTTPS. It's just an added bonus which happens to make your site even more secure.

There are other bonuses too:

- Sites in the Cloudflare network see significant performance increases. They are also less likely to come under spam attacks.
- Cloudflare offers free SSL certificates for those that want to migrate to an HTTPS connection.
- Setting up Cloudflare on your site is free, takes minutes, and costs nothing. And if you don't like it, it's just as easy to remove.

Cloudflare included in Web Hosting

When you log in to cPanel you may spot a Cloudflare icon:

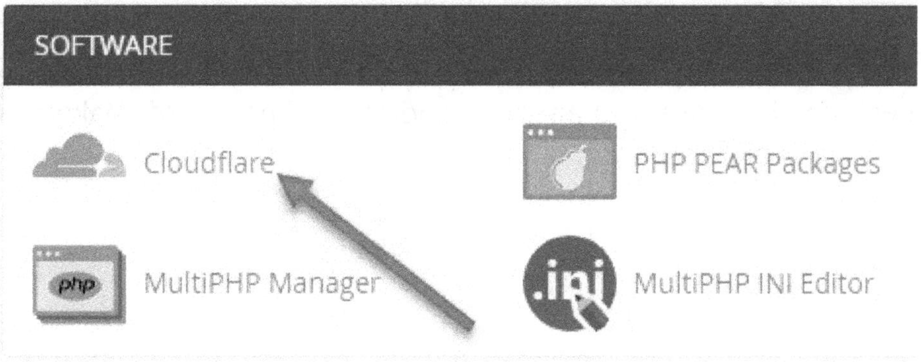
SOFTWARE
Cloudflare
PHP PEAR Packages
MultiPHP Manager
MultiPHP INI Editor

This means you can actually add your website to Cloudflare from within cPanel.

Alternatively, you can set up an account on the Cloudflare website and administer everything from there instead. That's the way I recommend you do this.

It's possible to work on Cloudflare from within cPanel AND the Cloudflare website at the same time. However, there are differences in the interface and things can soon get confusing. In this book, I'm going to assume you use the Cloudflare website for adding and managing your Cloudflare tasks.

OK, let's open an account on Cloudflare. This is the first step in the migration to HTTPS.

Create a Cloudflare account

Head on over to the Cloudflare website:

HTTPs://www.cloudflare.com/

Once there, click on the signup link.

The only details you will need to enter are an email address and password. Make sure you use a valid email and a strong password:

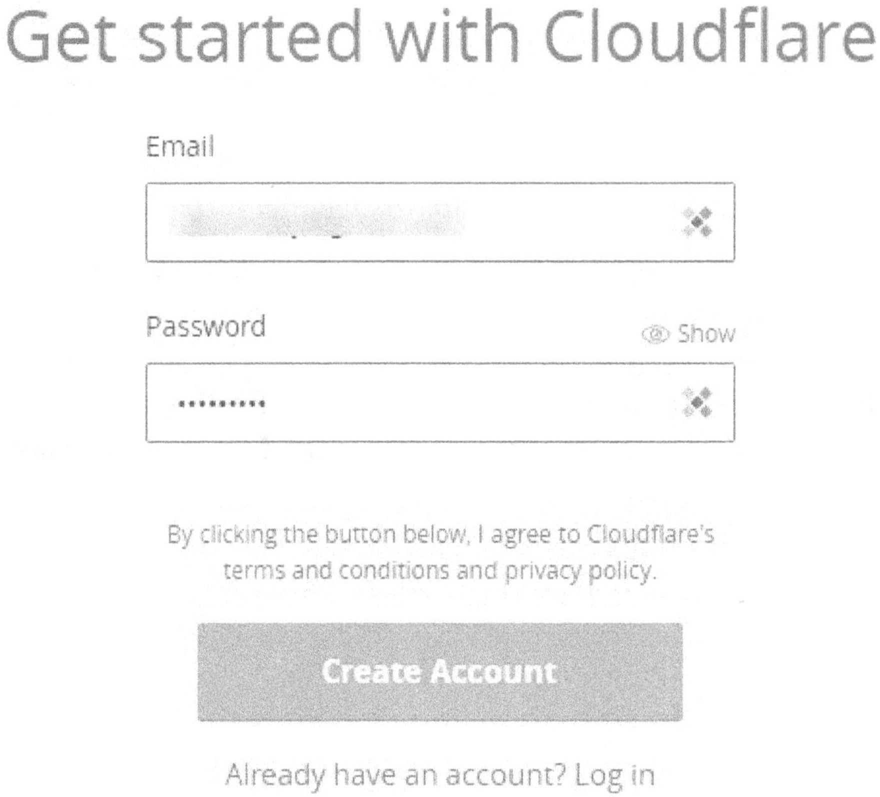
Get started with Cloudflare
Email
Password
Show
By clicking the button below, I agree to Cloudflare's terms and conditions and privacy policy.
Create Account
Already have an account? Log in

Once you enter an email and password, Cloudflare will ask for the site you want to add to its network.

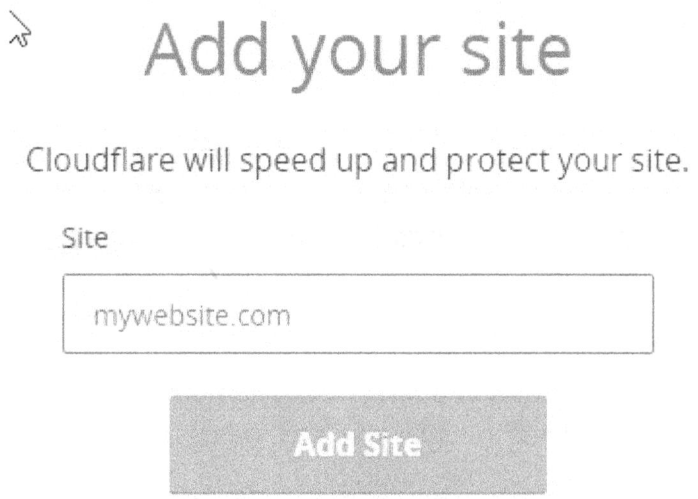
Add your site
Cloudflare will speed up and protect your site.
Site
mywebsite.com
Add Site

We'll do that in the next section. For now, take a look at the top right of your screen. You should be able to see your email address plus links to **Support** and **+Add Site**.

Your email address is actually a menu link. Click on it:

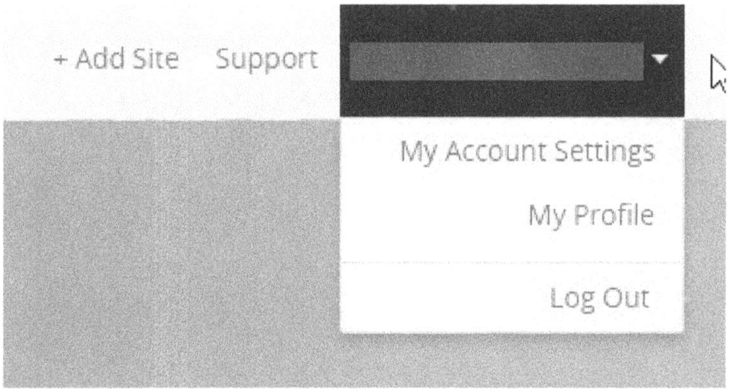
+ Add Site
Support
[redacted]
My Account Settings
My Profile
Log Out

You have access to your account settings and profile in that menu as well as a link to log out of the Cloudflare site.

The Account settings will show you a list of any paid add-ons in your account. You won't have anything there if you're just setting up the free SSL.

You can change your password and set up two-factor authentication on the profile page if you want to.

Now click the logout link to close your Cloudflare session. We'll add a site to your account in the next section.

Add your site

Head back to Cloudflare and log in.

Make sure you save your username and password if you haven't already done so. I personally use a password tool (Last Pass or Sticky Password are my favorites). A good PW manager remembers all my passwords for me. This is invaluable if you use really secure passwords (recommended).

You will see the same '**Add your site**' screen you saw earlier.

Obviously, this is a new account and you haven't added a site yet so Cloudflare prompts you to add one. After you add the first site you may want to add others to this account. In that case, you would simply click the **+Add Site** link in the top menu. That will bring you back to the same **Add your site** screen.

OK, let's add a site.

Enter your site domain and click the **Add Site** button.

Add your site
Cloudflare will speed up and protect your site.
Site
1
harlun.co.uk
2
Add Site

Cloudflare will take a few seconds to process the site. You'll then see a message: **We're querying your DNS records.**

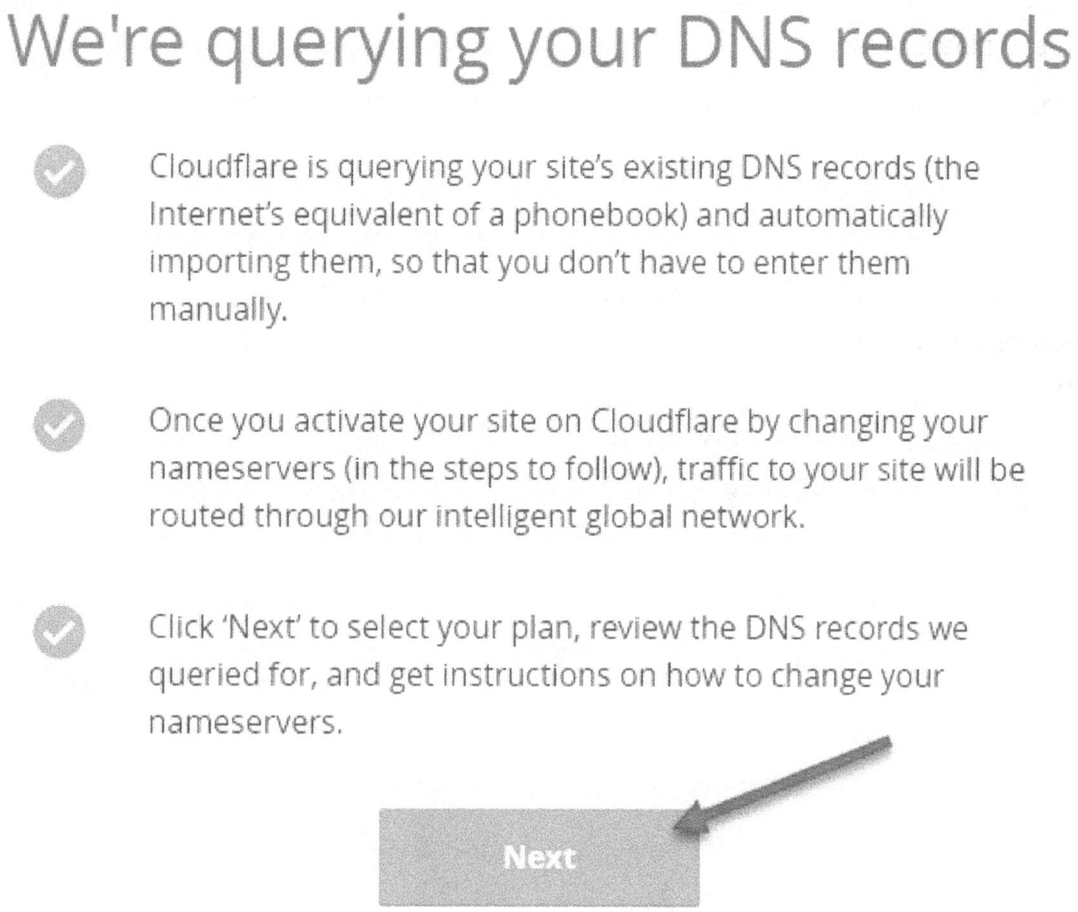
We're querying your DNS records
Cloudflare is querying your site's existing DNS records (the Internet's equivalent of a phonebook) and automatically importing them, so that you don't have to enter them manually.
Once you activate your site on Cloudflare by changing your nameservers (in the steps to follow), traffic to your site will be routed through our intelligent global network.
Click 'Next' to select your plan, review the DNS records we queried for, and get instructions on how to change your nameservers.
Next

Click on the **Next** button.

The system then asks which plan you want. There are currently four options:

Select a Plan
FREE
$0/month
per website
Includes:
Global CDN
Unmetered Mitigation of DDoS attacks
Free shared SSL certificate
PRO
$20/month
per website
All Free features, plus:
Web application firewall (WAF) with Cloudflare rulesets
Mobile & Image Optimizations
Additional Page Rules for fine-grained configuration
BUSINESS
$200/month
Prioritized Email Support
Custom SSL certs
ENTERPRISE
Get in Touch
All Business features, plus:
24/7/365 enterprise-grade phone, email, and chat support
Dedicated account team
100% uptime guarantee with 25x reimbursement SLA
Access to raw request logs
Learn More
1
2
Confirm Plan

Select the **Free** plan and click the **Confirm Plan** button.

The next screen has a lot of information on it. Cloudflare asks you to check if their list of “records” is complete. Only the most technical people will know what it all means. Don’t let it discourage you.

You'll see your domain listed as an A record with the Cloudflare status turned on:

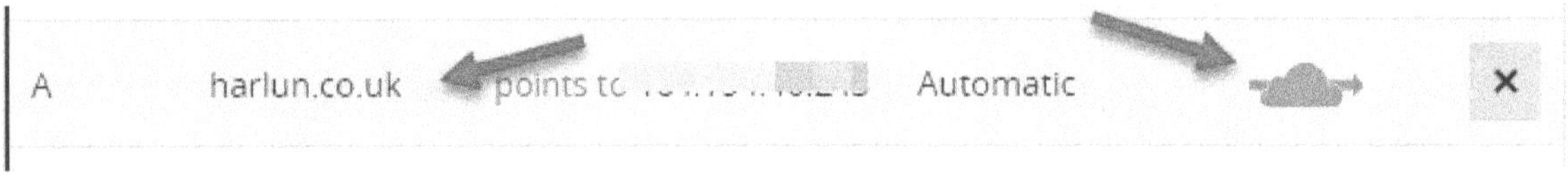
A
harlun.co.uk
points to
Automatic
×

You’ll also see a CNAME record type called www which has Cloudflare turned on. Those two records make sure Cloudflare protects your site. You will also have a few other records.

Scroll to the bottom and click **Continue**.

You'll be taken to a screen that asks you to change your Nameservers.

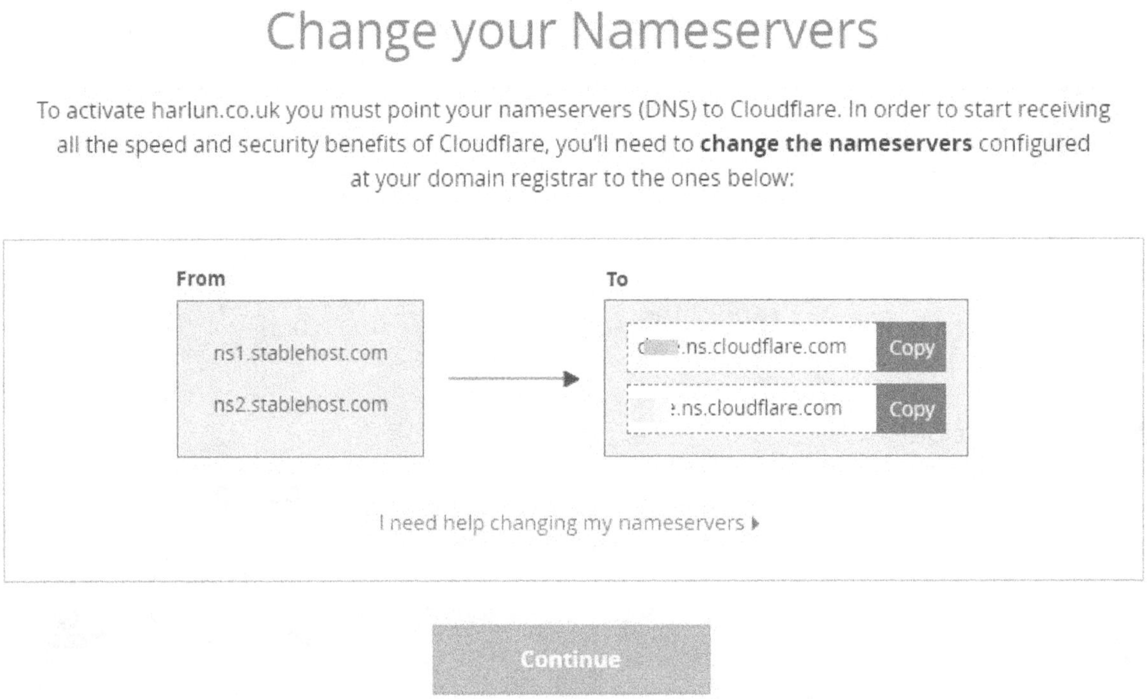
Change your Nameservers
To activate harlun.co.uk you must point your nameservers (DNS) to Cloudflare. In order to start receiving all the speed and security benefits of Cloudflare, you'll need to change the nameservers configured at your domain registrar to the ones below:
From
To
ns1.stablehost.com
ns2.stablehost.com
.ns.cloudflare.com
Copy
.ns.cloudflare.com
Copy
I need help changing my nameservers
Continue

Your domain name servers are most likely set to those of your web host. That means when someone visits your site your registrar automatically redirects them to your web host.

However, we need visitors auto-directed to Cloudflare first. Cloudflare will then filter the traffic as we saw earlier. It then forwards the "good" traffic to the nearest “copy” of your website on the global network.

The next step is to change the DNS to bring Cloudflare into play. We’ll continue with this in the next section. For now, leave the **Change your Nameservers** screen open.

Change DNS at the registrar

You need to have access to your domain registrar to change the DNS. This will be Namecheap if you followed my recommendations. If you use a different registrar that's fine but I'll show you the process in Namecheap as that's the one I use.

NOTE: You may be using your web host as registrar. That's quite common as hosts want to be your registrar as well. It is not something I recommend but it is your choice. If you're not using Namecheap and cannot find where to change the DNS, please ask your registrar for guidance.

DNS Change on Namecheap

Login to Namecheap.

You will see a list of your domains. Find the one you just added to Cloudflare and click the **Manage** button to the right of the domain name.

harlun.co.uk
ACTIVE
Expiring
Jun 16, 2021
MANAGE

When you scroll down the page you'll see the **Nameservers** section:

NAMESERVERS
Custom DNS
ns1.stablehost.com
ns2.stablehost.com
ADD NAMESERVER

Mine currently shows the Stablehost name servers.

Now edit the Nameservers to the ones given to you in Cloudflare:

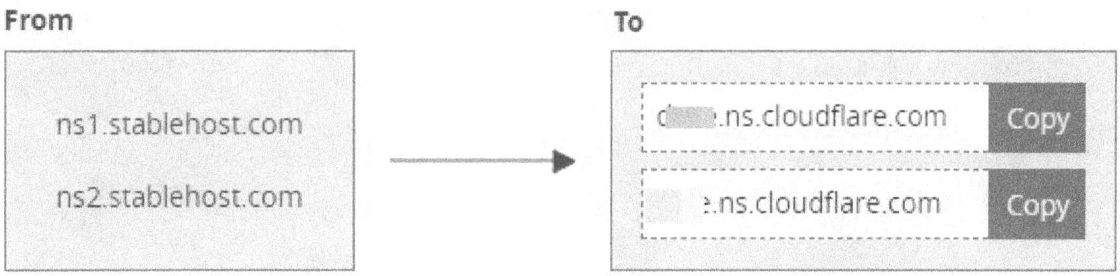
From
To
ns1.stablehost.com
ns2.stablehost.com
Copy
Copy

Once you enter these into Namecheap you'll see a small menu appear with a check mark to save your data:

NAMESERVERS
Custom DNS
ns.cloudflare.com
ns.cloudflare.com
ADD NAMESERVER

Click the check mark to save.

You will now get a message (or two) at the top of the screen:

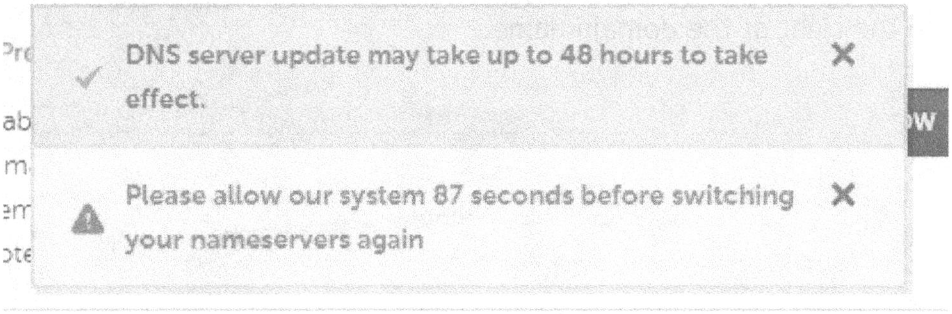
DNS server update may take up to 48 hours to take effect.
Please allow our system 87 seconds before switching your nameservers again

The first message says that it can take up to 48 hours before the nameservers are fully updated. Don't worry, your site won't go down during that time. What it will do is switch between the old and new nameservers until the changeover is final. In reality, I usually see the change happening within an hour. That may also be due to my geographical location so mileage may vary here.

Back on the Cloudflare site, click **Continue** at the bottom of the **Change your Nameservers** screen:

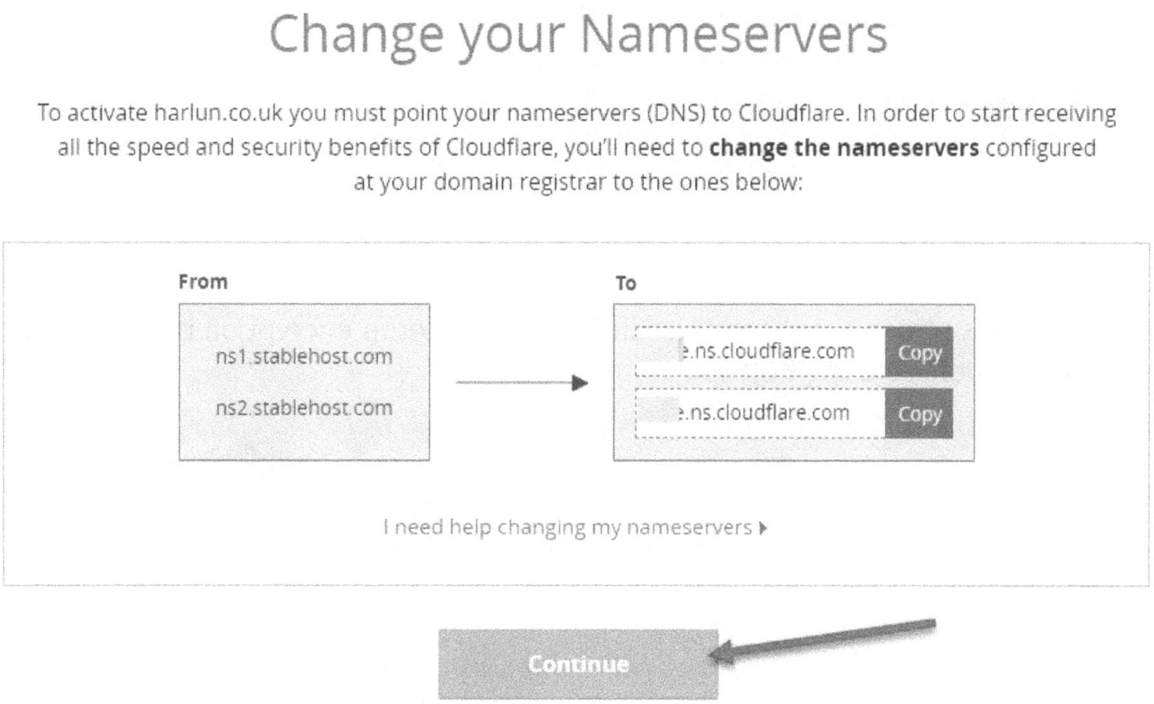
Change your Nameservers
To activate harlun.co.uk you must point your nameservers (DNS) to Cloudflare. In order to start receiving all the speed and security benefits of Cloudflare, you'll need to change the nameservers configured at your domain registrar to the ones below:
From
ns1.stablehost.com
ns2.stablehost.com
To
.ns.cloudflare.com
Copy
.ns.cloudflare.com
Copy
I need help changing my nameservers
Continue

What you see next depends on whether the Nameserver change has completed in your geographical location. This is what I see:

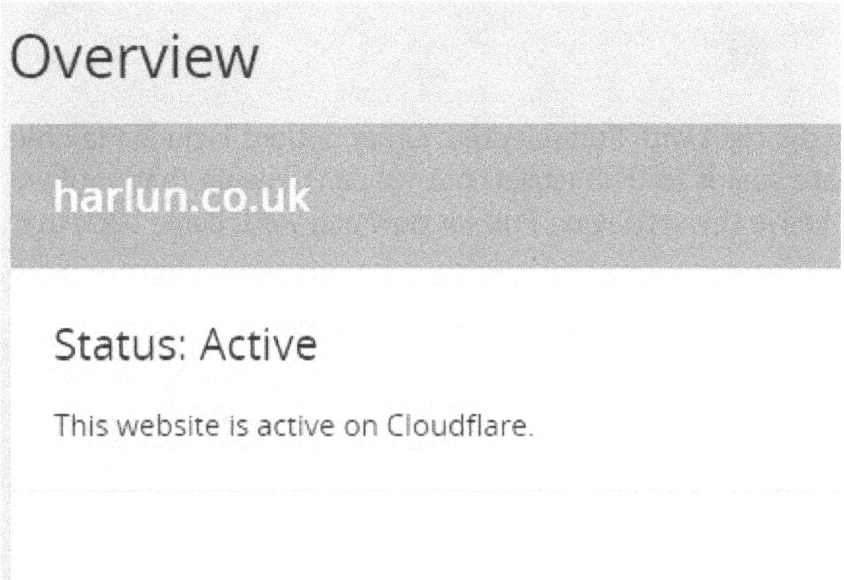
Overview
harlun.co.uk
Status: Active
This website is active on Cloudflare.

My site is already active on Cloudflare. You can keep the screen open and refresh it periodically until your site is active if you want to. Or, you can log out of Cloudflare and come back later if you prefer.

Check your Edge certificate

Now that the site is active on Cloudflare we should be able to check that an **Edge Certificate** has been created.

Click on the **Crypto** link in the menu across the top:

Overview
DNS
Crypto
Firewall

At the top of this screen you'll see that Cloudflare has setup encryption between your website and Cloudflare using **Full SSL:**

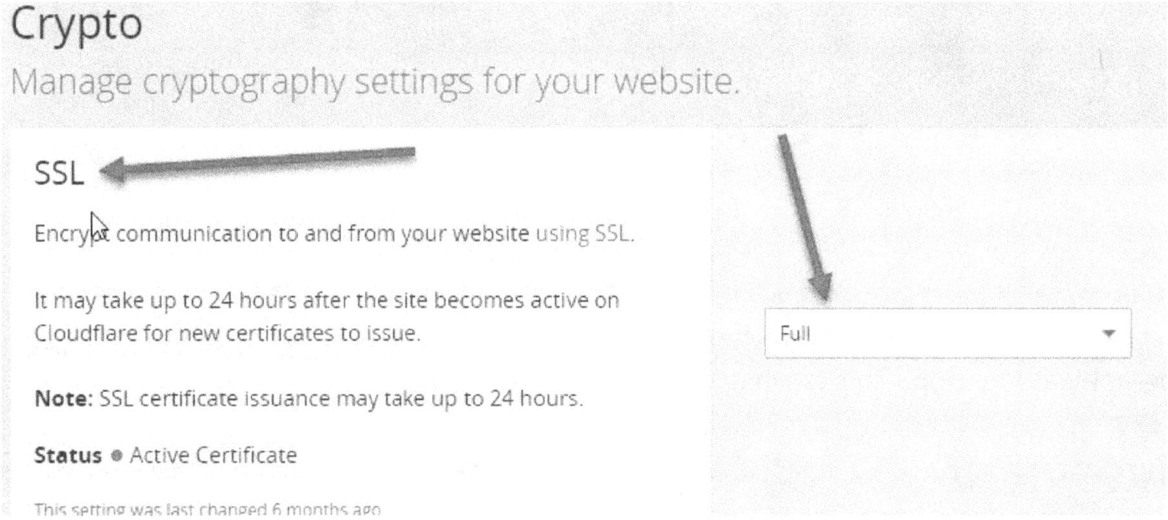
Crypto
Manage cryptography settings for your website.
SSL
communication to and from your website using SSL.
It may take up to 24 hours after the site becomes active on Cloudflare for new certificates to issue.
Note: SSL certificate issuance may take up to 24 hours.
Status ● Active Certificate
Full

There is a drop-down box on the right with **Full** selected. Other options include **Flexible** and **Full (strict)**. Our ultimate goal is for Full (strict) but we can't enable that until we have the origin certificate. Leave the setting on **Full** for now and we'll come back to it later.

Scroll down the page until you get to the **Edge Certificates** section.

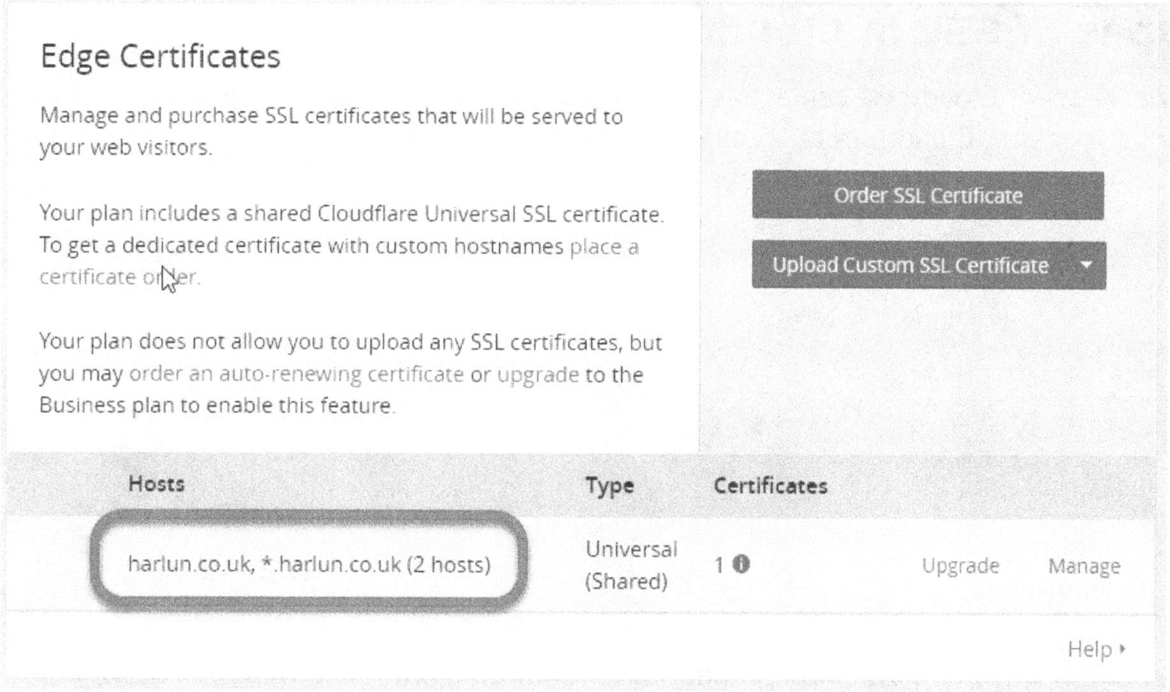
Edge Certificates
Manage and purchase SSL certificates that will be served to your web visitors.
Your plan includes a shared Cloudflare Universal SSL certificate. To get a dedicated certificate with custom hostnames place a certificate order.
Your plan does not allow you to upload any SSL certificates, but you may order an auto-renewing certificate or upgrade to the Business plan to enable this feature.
Order SSL Certificate
Upload Custom SSL Certificate
Hosts
Type
Certificates
harlun.co.uk, *.harlun.co.uk (2 hosts)
Universal (Shared)
1
Upgrade
Manage
Help

You should see your domain added with "two hosts". This will essentially cover any requests for your site with and without "www" plus any subdomains.

If you don't see the edge certificate you have to wait until it shows. It will be visible as soon as Cloudflare has added your site to its network.

OK, that's it. Your site will now "pass" through Cloudflare, with all the benefits that include. We now need to set up the SSL certificate to secure the site. We'll look at the types of SSL offered by Cloudflare in the next chapter.

Types of SSL in Cloudflare

As we've seen, Cloudflare can act as a filter for your website. When a user comes along to visit your site, Cloudflare takes over and checks whether it's safe to give them access. If they don't pose a threat they are free to browse your website.

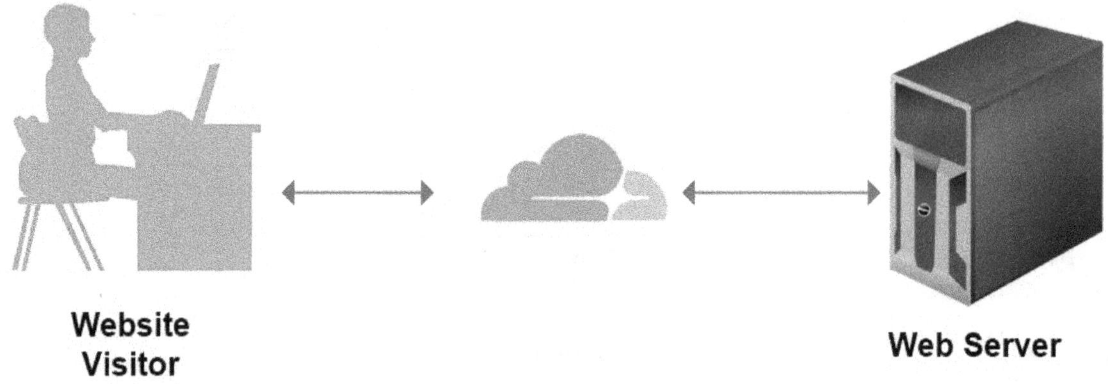
Website
Visitor
Web Server

In this diagram, there are two "connections" required to view the website. There is the user to Cloudflare, and then Cloudflare to the web server. Cloudflare is the intermediary, controlling who gets through.

So far, this is nothing to do with HTTPS or a secure website. For that, we need an SSL certificate. We have a few options here so let's look at each of those in turn.

Option 1. Flexible SSL

Flexible SSL is one of the easier systems to get up and running.

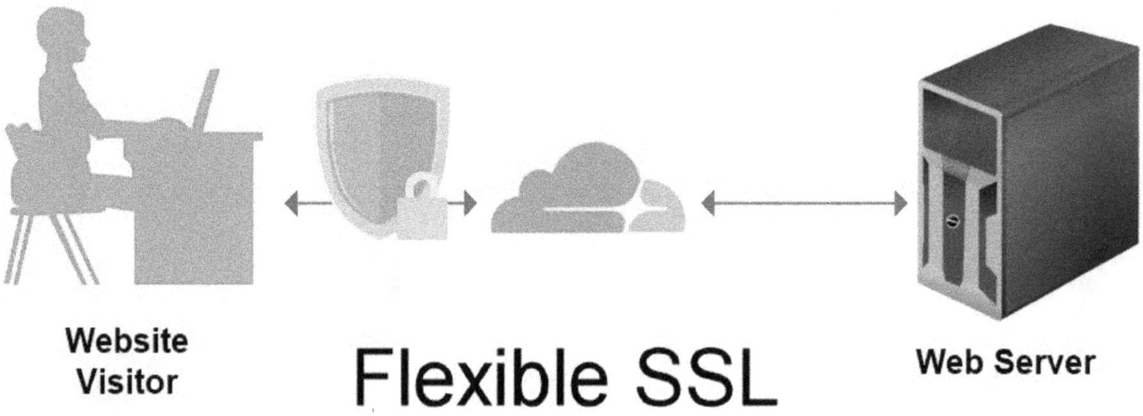
Website
Visitor
Flexible SSL
Web Server

In Flexible SSL there is a certificate between the user and Cloudflare. This certificate keeps the connection between the user and Cloudflare secure. However, there isn't a certificate between Cloudflare and the server so that connection is not secure.

The advantage is that you don't need an actual certificate on your server for visitors to see a secure connection status. This is because their connection to Cloudflare is secure.

Flexible SSL is better than nothing but it doesn't provide maximum security. That's where the second option comes in.

Option 2. Full SSL

In Full SSL, there's also a certificate to secure data between Cloudflare and the web server.

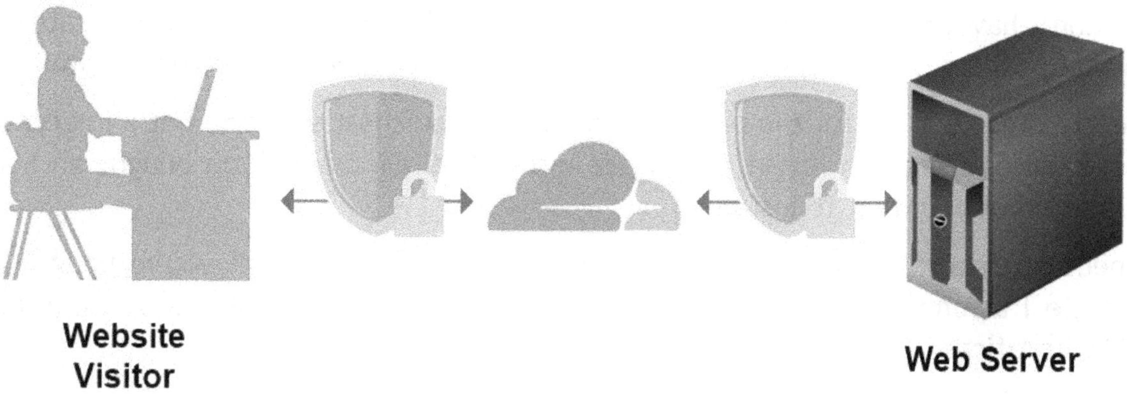
Website
Visitor
Web Server

There is a problem though. In Full SSL, the connection between Cloudflare and the web server is not authenticated. Cloudflare gives us a third option to fix this.

Option 3. Full SSL (Strict)

Full SSL (Strict) is the same diagram as we've just seen:

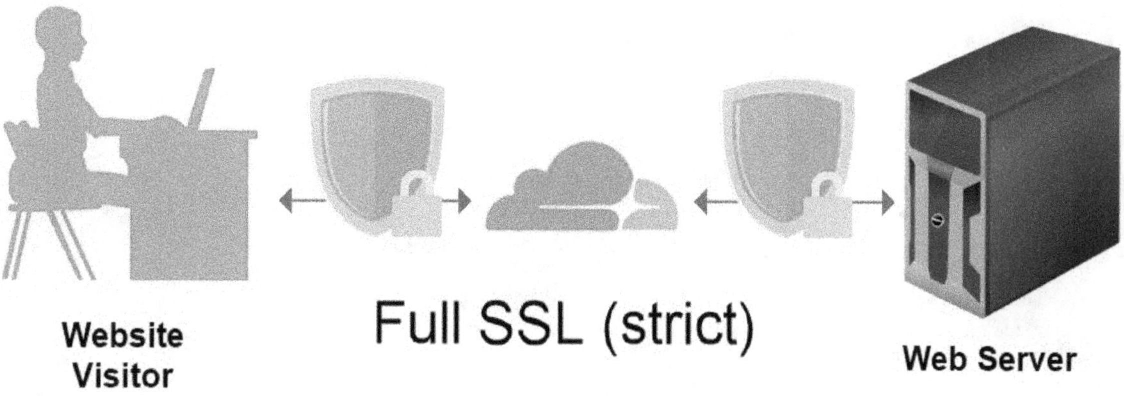
Website
Visitor
Full SSL (strict)
Web Server

The difference here is that the certificate between Cloudflare and the server is now authenticated as well. This is the type of SSL you really want to set up. It's also the type of SLL we'll set up in this book.

As you can see from the diagram we need two certificates for maximum security.

The first one sits between the user and Cloudflare (Edge certificate). Cloudflare creates this certificate for us automatically and installs it.

The second certificate sits between Cloudflare and the server. This one is the origin certificate.

What you do next will depend on whether you have (and want to use) AutoSSL.

If you intend to use AutoSSL, then the AutoSSL creates the origin certificate between Cloudflare and the server.

If you don't have, or don't want to use AutoSSL, we will create an origin certificate to sit in that position. Actually, Cloudflare creates it for us. All we need to do is install it.

There are other options for the origin certificate. If your host supports **Let's Encrypt**, you can easily create an origin certificate using that. Or maybe you bought an SSL certificate that you want to install.

You need to choose an origin certificate before we can proceed. If you've bought a certificate I assume you'll want to use that. For everyone else, decide between an AutoSSL certificate and a Cloudflare origin certificate.

Choosing an origin certificate

Do you have AutoSSL or a certificate already assigned? If you do, then the easiest solution is to use that. But do be aware that these have short renewal periods. This shouldn't be a problem since they auto-renew but I've had a few issues with AutoSSL certificates not renewing properly. I recommend you set a reminder for the expiry date if you decide to use an AutoSSL certificate. This way you can check it has renewed OK. If you don't want the hassle of checking auto-renewal then go with a Cloudflare origin certificate.

It's worth remembering that you can change the origin certificate at any time. I will show you how to do this later in the book. If you're on the fence about this then use AutoSSL for now. If it continues to renew OK, then stick with it. If there are problems and you don't want the worry then change to a Cloudflare certificate. Cloudflare origin certificates have one big advantage over AutoSSL generated certificates. They are valid for 15 years!

There isn't a choice if you don't have AutoSSL available to you. In this case, simply go with a Cloudflare origin certificate.

SECTION 1 - If Using AutoSSL

You already have your edge certificate since AutoSSL created and installed this for you. You can go to Section 3 in this book if you want to stick with the cPanel generated certificate.

SECTION 2 - IF Using Cloudflare Origin

There are a few steps we need to follow to install and use the 15-year Origin Certificate from Cloudflare.

1. Uninstall AutoSSL installed certificates.
2. Exclude your domain from AutoSSL so that cPanel doesn't try to renew the origin certificate.
3. Generate the new Origin Certificate.
4. Install the Origin Certificate on your server.

After completing these steps, we'll be in a position to switch SSL to Full (strict) and test that everything works. It probably won't, but don't worry. I'll show you how to fix any common problems.

Let's get started.

Uninstall cPanel generated certificates

AutoSSL generated and installed an origin certificate on our server and we need to remove it.

Login to cPanel and scroll down to the **SECURITY** section. You're looking for the **SSL/TLS** icon

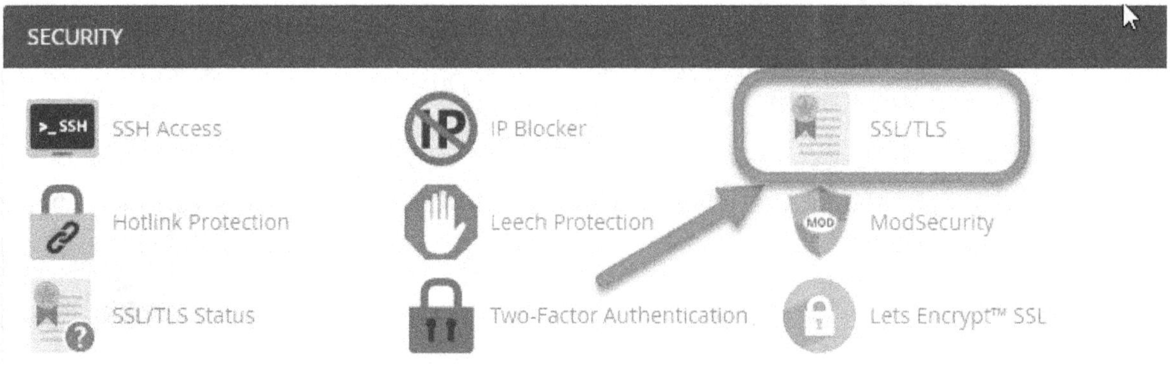
SECURITY
SSH Access
IP Blocker
SSL/TLS
Hotlink Protection
Leech Protection
ModSecurity
SSL/TLS Status
Two-Factor Authentication
Lets Encrypt™ SSL

Click on it.

On the SSL/TLS screen, click on the bottom option **Install and Manage SSL for your site (HTTPS):**

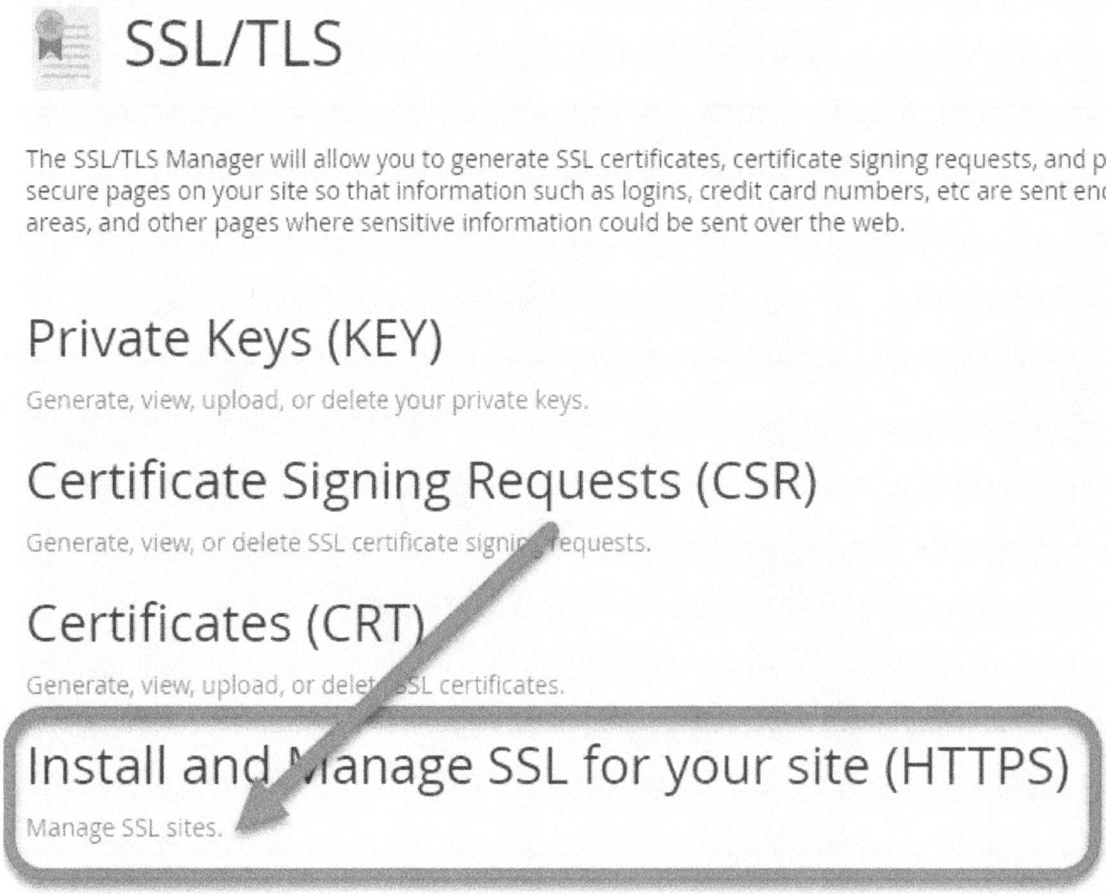
SSL/TLS
The SSL/TLS Manager will allow you to generate SSL certificates, certificate signing requests, and private
secure pages on your site so that information such as logins, credit card numbers, etc are sent encrypte
areas, and other pages where sensitive information could be sent over the web.
Private Keys (KEY)
Generate, view, upload, or delete your private keys.
Certificate Signing Requests (CSR)
Certificates (CRT)
Install and Manage SSL for your site (HTTPS)
Manage SSL sites.

You will see a list of all your domains on the server. Locate the one you're working on. You'll recognize it because it will have both the www and non-www versions of your domain listed:

cpanel.harlun.co.uk
harlun.cheebles.com
harlun.co.uk
mail.harlun.co.uk
webdisk.harlun.co.uk
webmail.harlun.co.uk
www.harlun.cheebles.com
www.harlun.co.uk

To the far right of this table is the **Actions** column:

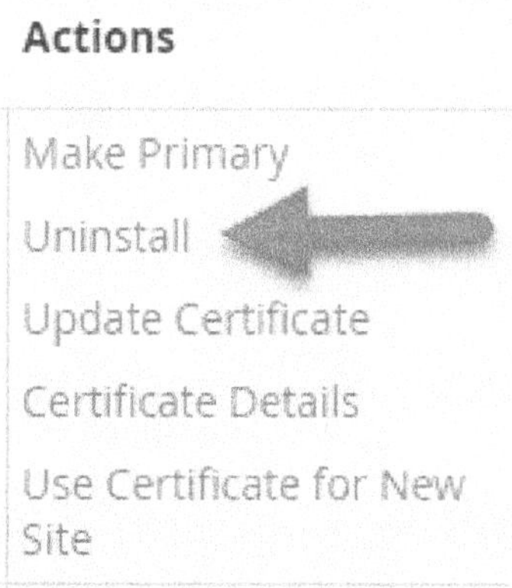
Actions
Make Primary
Uninstall
Update Certificate
Certificate Details
Use Certificate for New Site

Click on the **Uninstall** link to uninstall the cPanel generated certificate.

A message will ask you to confirm that you want to delete the SSL host as this action cannot be undone. Click the **Proceed** button.

Your domains origin certificate will be removed from your server.

Click the button on the top left to go back to the main cPanel:

stablehost
SSL/TLS
Manage SSL Hosts
This interface lets you configure SSL for your domains.
An SSL certificate can secure one or more domains; to c
file that must also be present to install the certificate. S
server; in the event that the server cannot find the requ

Exclude domain from AutoSSL

With the certificate deleted, we now need to stop AutoSSL from trying to renew it.

Scroll down to the **SECURITY** section again and click on **SSL/TLS Status**:

SECURITY
>_SSH
SSH Access
Hotlink Protecti
SSL/TLS Status

At the top of the screen is a search box. Use it to search for your domain name:

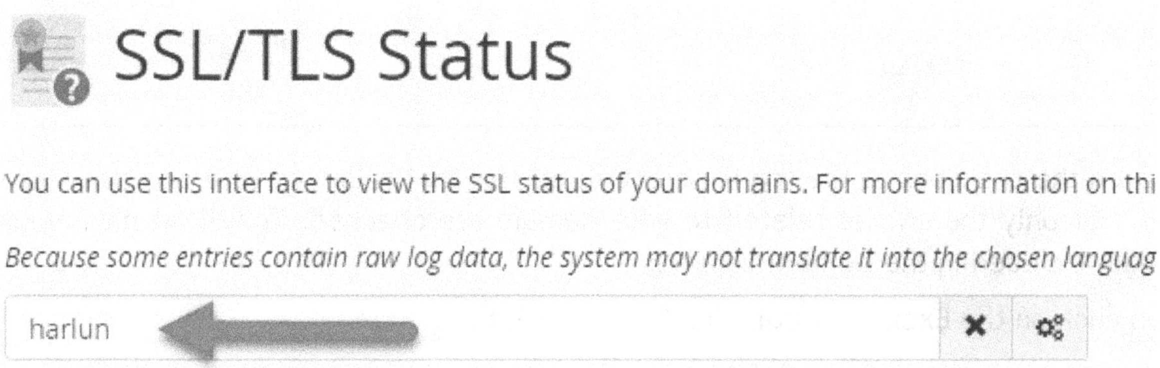
SSL/TLS Status
You can use this interface to view the SSL status of your domains. For more information on thi
Because some entries contain raw log data, the system may not translate it into the chosen languag
harlun

You will see a list of entries related to your domain and the AutoSSL status. I have eight entries in this list.

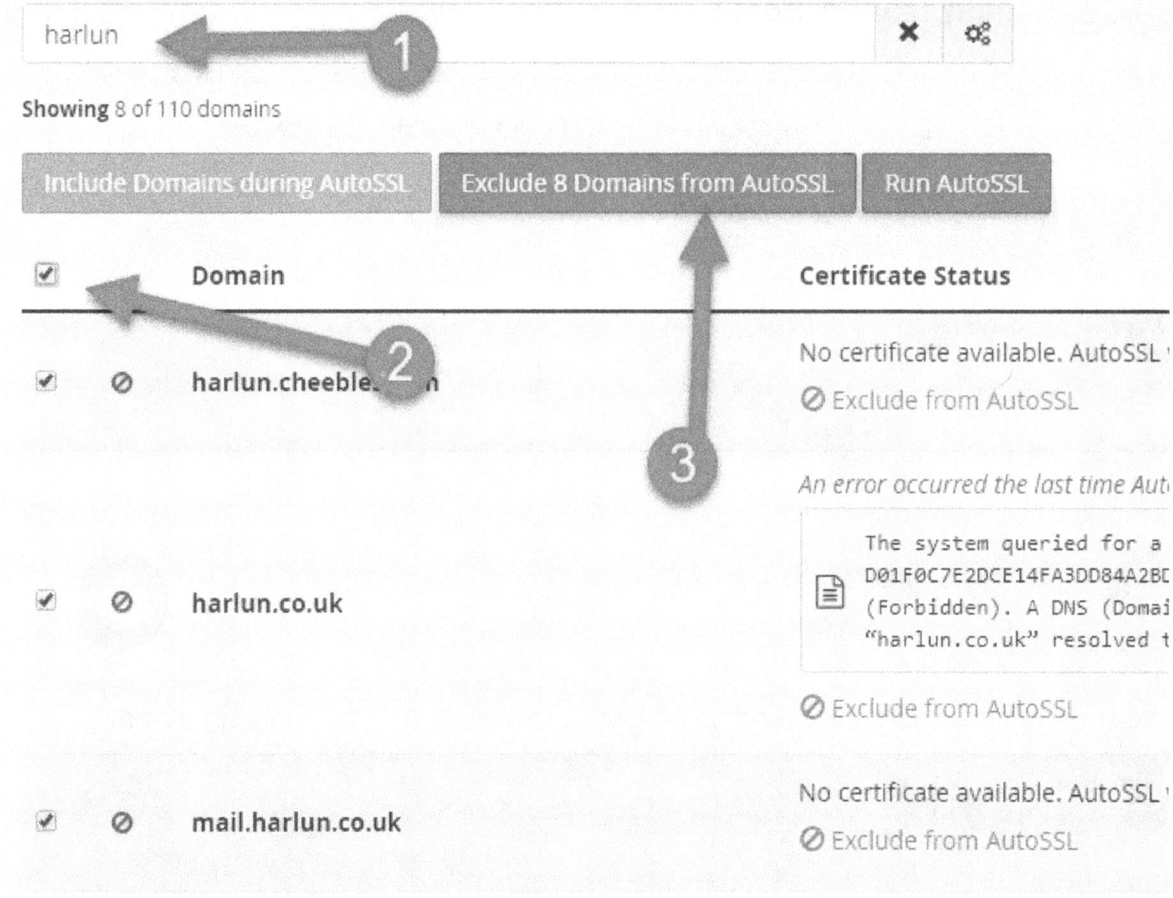
harlun
1
Showing 8 of 110 domains
Include Domains during AutoSSL
Exclude 8 Domains from AutoSSL
Run AutoSSL
Domain
Certificate Status
2
3
harlun.co.uk
mail.harlun.co.uk
No certificate available. AutoSSL
Exclude from AutoSSL
An error occurred the last time Aut
The system queried for a
D01F0C7E2DCE14FA3DD84A2BC
(Forbidden). A DNS (Domai
"harlun.co.uk" resolved t

Click on the checkbox at the top to select all entries that relate to your domain. Make sure that only the entries related to your domain are checked. They'll all have your domain included in the **Domain** column.

Then click on the **Exclude X Domains from AutoSSL**.

You will get a message that all domains will now be excluded from the AutoSSL service and renewal.

Delete existing origin certificates for this domain

Although we don't have to, I still think a good idea to delete existing certificates for the domain in question. You can skip this step if you want to.

There may be several certificates depending on how long the site was running on AutoSSL.

In cPanel, scroll down to the **Security** section and click on **SSL/TLS**.

Now click on the **Certificates (CRT)** link:

Private Keys (KEY)

Generate, view, upload, or delete your private keys.

Certificate Signing Requests (CSR)

Generate, view, or delete SSL certificate signing requests.

Certificates (CRT)

Generate, view, upload, or delete SSL certificates.

Install and Manage SSL for your site (HTTPS)

Manage SSL sites.

You can view all the certificates on your server in this screen. The ones we're looking for are older certificates issued for our domain.

I have found four on my server. cPanel issued these and they've either expired already or due to expire in the coming weeks:

harlun.co.uk harlun.cheebles.com mail.harlun.co.uk webdisk.harlun.co.uk www.harlun.cheebles.com www.harlun.co.uk	cPanel, Inc.	5/14/18	2048	Cert for "harlun.cheebles.com" 1518418924.0	Edit Install	Delete
harlun.co.uk harlun.cheebles.com mail.harlun.co.uk webdisk.harlun.co.uk www.harlun.cheebles.com www.harlun.co.uk	cPanel, Inc.	2/27/18	2048	Cert for "harlun.cheebles.com" 1511854384.0	Edit Install	Delete
harlun.co.uk harlun.cheebles.com mail.harlun.co.uk webdisk.harlun.co.uk www.harlun.cheebles.com www.harlun.co.uk	cPanel, Inc.	12/12/17	2048	Cert for "harlun.cheebles.com" 1	Edit Install	Delete
harlun.co.uk harlun.cheebles.com mail.harlun.co.uk www.harlun.cheebles.com www.harlun.co.uk	cPanel, Inc.	12/8/17	2048	Cert for "harlun.cheebles.com"	Edit Install	Delete

I can safely delete all these certificates.

For each entry, click the **Delete** button next to the listing. Make sure you only delete the ones related to your current domain.

We can proceed once you delete the old certificates.

At this stage, if you go over to your domain using the HTTPS it won't load. You should get an error message saying something went wrong—or similar. Here's the message on my site:

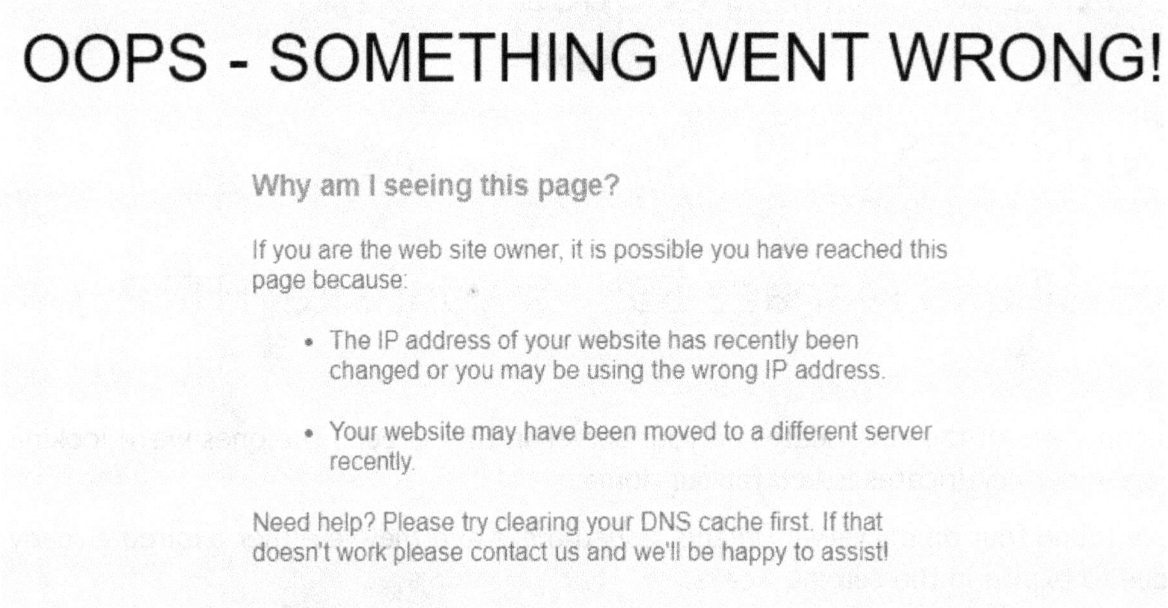
OOPS - SOMETHING WENT WRONG!
Why am I seeing this page?
If you are the web site owner, it is possible you have reached this page because:
The IP address of your website has recently been changed or you may be using the wrong IP address.
Your website may have been moved to a different server recently.
Need help? Please try clearing your DNS cache first. If that doesn't work please contact us and we'll be happy to assist!

Our site is still running on the Cloudflare network, but remember earlier we saw that the SSL was set to **Full**. Full SSL requires an origin certificate and we just deleted that. We can restore the HTTPS right now by selecting Flexible SSL. Remember, Flexible SSL does not require an origin certificate, just an edge certificate, which is on the server.

Let's do that now.

Login to Cloudflare and click on the **Crypto** tab.

In the SSL section, select **Flexible**. This change may take a while to switch over. Once it does the HTTPs version of your site should be back up and running. You might need to clear your browser cache.

However, our goal is not to implement flexible SSL. We want Full (strict), so let's keep going and generate an **Origin Certificate** we can use.

Generate an origin certificate

For Full (strict) SSL, we need to have a valid origin certificate. We can get Cloudflare to generate one for us.

Login to Cloudflare and select your domain (if you have more than one they'll appear in a list).

Click on the **Crypto** tab.

This is a familiar screen that shows the SSL method we're currently using. Mine is still set to **Flexible** from the last chapter but yours may be on **Full**.

You can see your **Edge Certificate** listed further down this screen.

Keep scrolling down until you see the **Origin Certificates** section.

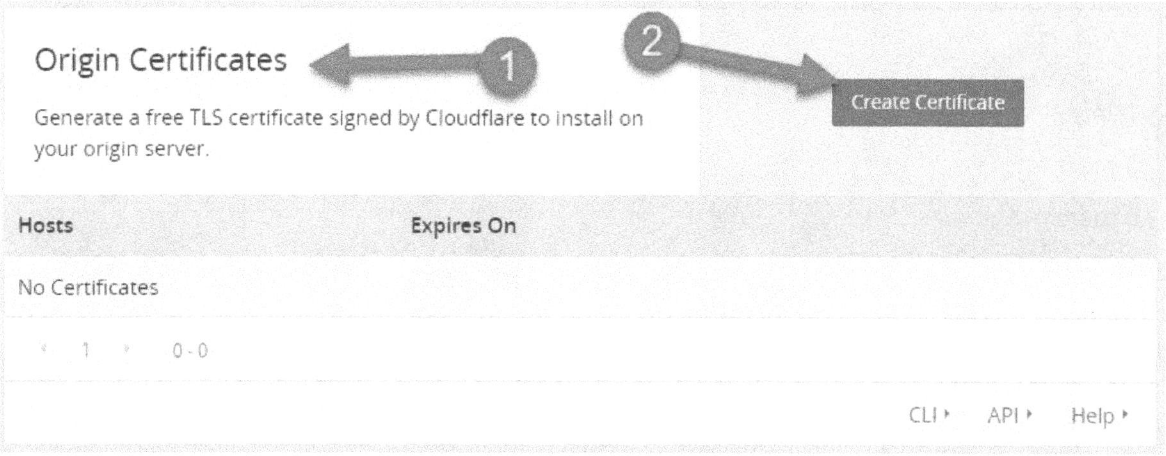
Origin Certificates
1
2
Create Certificate
Generate a free TLS certificate signed by Cloudflare to install on your origin server.
Hosts
Expires On
No Certificates
1
0 - 0
CLI
API
Help

There won't be an origin certificate listed yet so let's create one now.

Click on the **Create Certificate** button.

A popup screen will open. At the top, leave it set to **Let Cloudflare generate a private key and a CSR.**

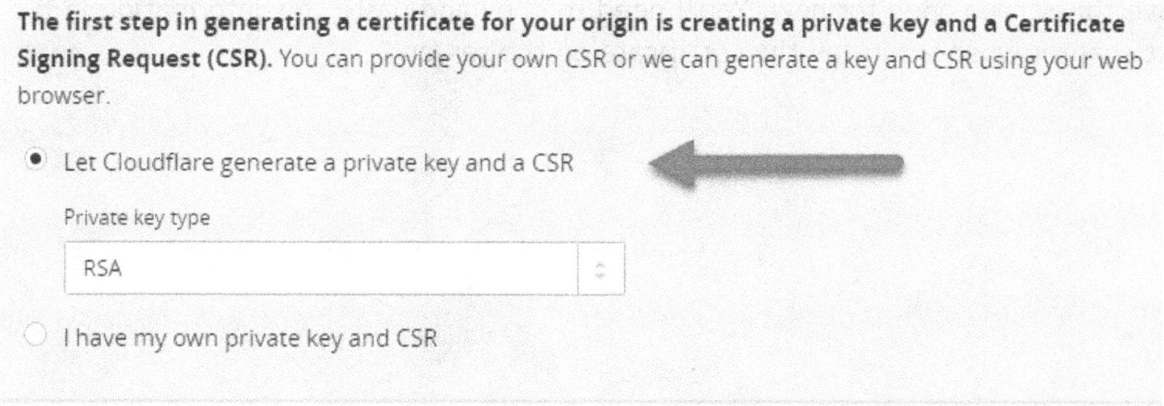
The first step in generating a certificate for your origin is creating a private key and a Certificate Signing Request (CSR). You can provide your own CSR or we can generate a key and CSR using your web browser.
Let Cloudflare generate a private key and a CSR
Private key type
RSA
I have my own private key and CSR

Under here you'll see the list of hostnames prefilled for you. It should include your domain name and a wildcard (*) version.

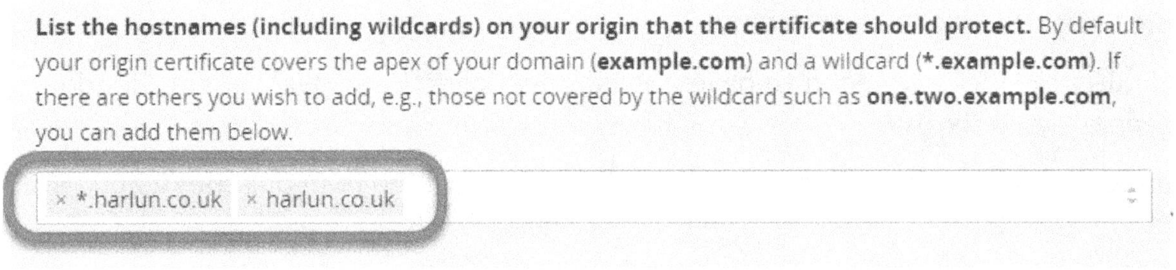
List the hostnames (including wildcards) on your origin that the certificate should protect. By default your origin certificate covers the apex of your domain (example.com) and a wildcard (*.example.com). If there are others you wish to add, e.g., those not covered by the wildcard such as one.two.example.com, you can add them below.
× *.harlun.co.uk
× harlun.co.uk

At the very bottom, you can choose how long you want the certificate to last before it expires. The default is 15 years. You can choose a shorter period if you have good reason to do so:

7 days
30 days
90 days
1 year
2 years
3 years
15 years
15 years

Once you've made your selection click the **Next** button. Cloudflare will now create your certificate and display it on the screen.

There will be two main parts to the certificate: the **origin certificate** and a **private key**.

Leave this screen open for now. You'll need to copy and paste this information in the next chapter when we install the certificate on the server.

Install the origin certificate

We created a Cloudflare origin certificate and a private key in the previous chapter. We're now going to install those on our server. It's usually a two-step process where we install the key first, then the certificate.

Let's do that now.

Upload the Private Key

Login to your cPanel and scroll down to the **Security** section.

Click on the **SSL/TLS** icon.

To upload the **Private Key**, click on the first option:

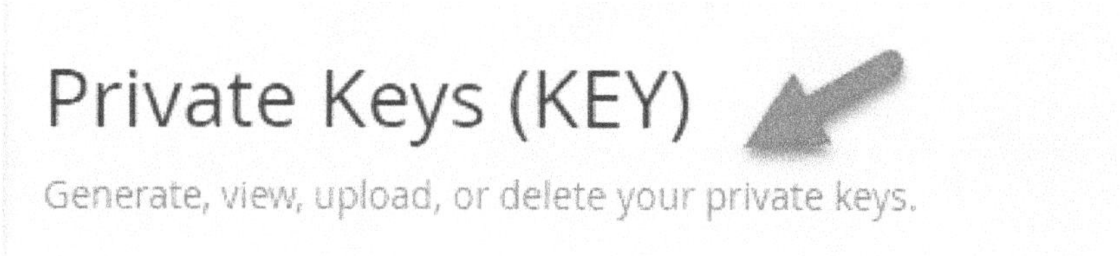
Private Keys (KEY)
Generate, view, upload, or delete your private keys.

You will see a number of keys are already on the server. Scroll past them and find the **Upload a New Private Key** section.

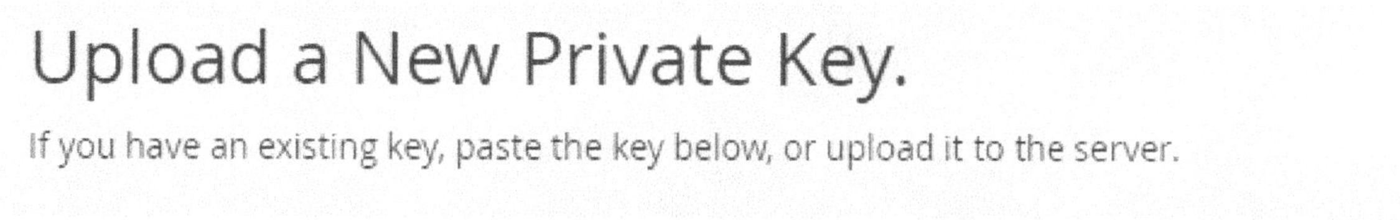
Upload a New Private Key.
If you have an existing key, paste the key below, or upload it to the server.

You will see two boxes. One is for the key itself and the other for a description.

Head back to the Cloudflare page we kept open. Now copy the entire **Private Key**, including -----BEGIN PRIVATE KEY----- and -----END PRIVATE KEY-----.

NOTE: Make sure you copy the Private Key, not the Certificate.

-----BEGIN PRIVATE KEY-----
MIIEvgIBADANBgkqhkiG9w0BAQEFAASCBKgwggSkAgEAAoIBAQCikamfnQrq9p46
BXi91tQN8nX4EThVSko2PafheYmvva01dcLJjcpvfxc1ys+U07GnB351w1bp/Dpw
hrboG1Xzmhw8rxrMT20mbPNqKa9WqMGo5P95a69YQ5dY3viDPo2K84LGsjzImbqu
wvl4eUre44L9yMQTI+nv+d8b7wapk7VXiIbb5SzG02F4eaRQm0/7R3/Mx158Rpjx
HYKLFq+tPTT81UUuPIxDOpBQ
-----END PRIVATE KEY-----

Back in cPanel, paste the Private Key in the correct box and enter a short description (I just use the domain name for this).

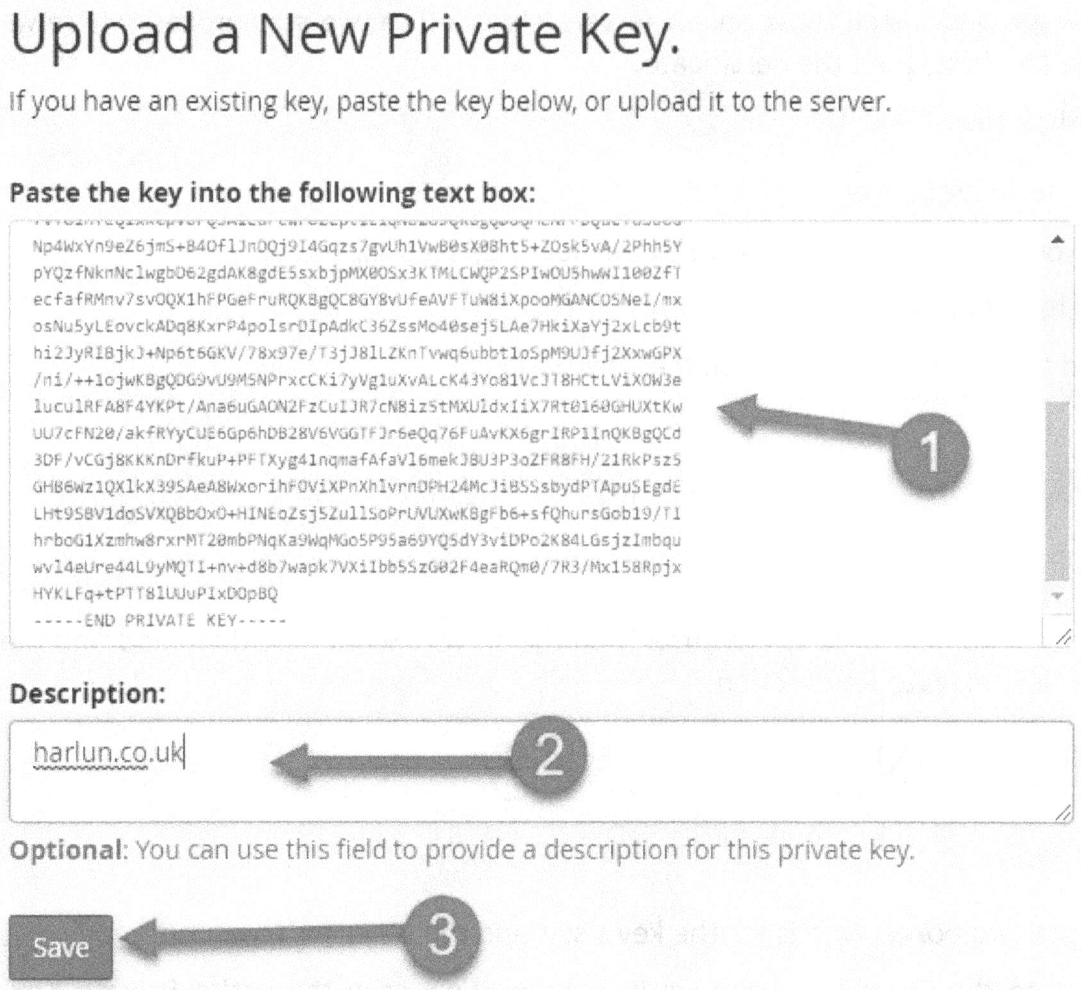
Upload a New Private Key.
If you have an existing key, paste the key below, or upload it to the server.
Paste the key into the following text box:
-----END PRIVATE KEY-----
1
Description:
harlun.co.uk
2
Optional: You can use this field to provide a description for this private key.
Save
3

Now click on the **Save** button.

You should get a confirmation message to say the key was installed correctly:

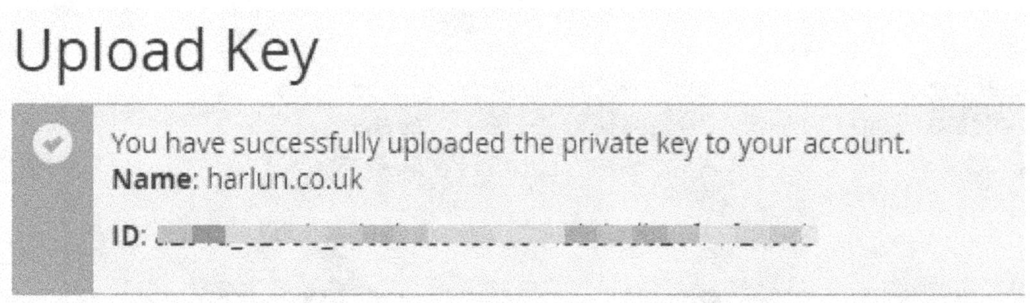
Upload Key
You have successfully uploaded the private key to your account.
Name: harlun.co.uk
ID:

We now need to install the certificate.

Upload Origin Certificate

Go back to the cPanel dashboard and click on **SSL/TLS** in the **SECURITY** section.

You now need to select the third option **Certificates (CRT)**.

Certificates (CRT)
Generate, view, upload, or delete SSL certificates.

Once the page loads you'll see all the certificates on the server. Scroll to the bottom to find the **Upload a New Certificate** section:

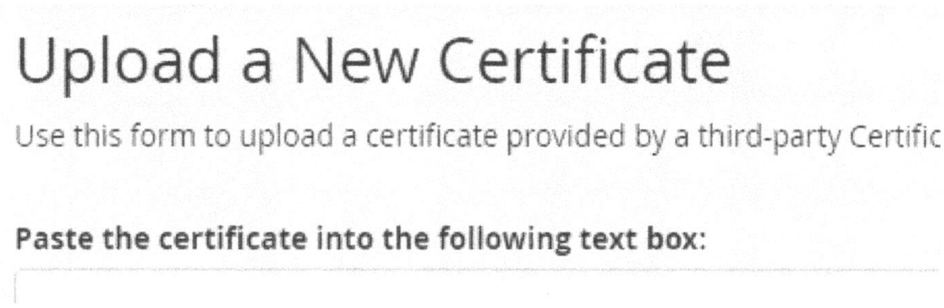
Upload a New Certificate
Use this form to upload a certificate provided by a third-party Certific
Paste the certificate into the following text box:

Again, there is a section for both certificate and description.

Go back to Cloudflare and copy the entire **Origin Certificate** including the -----BEGIN CERTIFICATE----- and -----END CERTIFICATE-----:

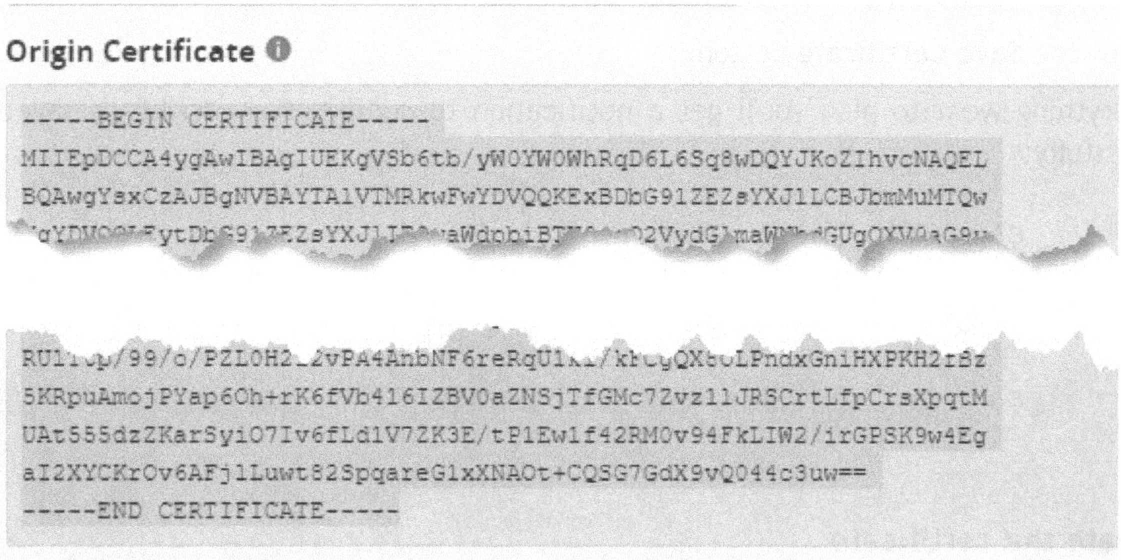
Origin Certificate
-----BEGIN CERTIFICATE-----
MIIEpDCCA4ygAwIBAgIUEKgVSb6tb/yW0YW0WhRqD6L6Sq8wDQYJKoZIhvcNAQEL
BQAwgYsxCzAJBgNVBAYTAlVTMRkwFwYDVQQKExBDbG91ZEZsYXJlLCBJbmMuMTQw
5KRpuAmojPYap6Oh+rK6fVb416IZBV0aZNSjTfGMc7Zvz1lJRSCrtLfpCrsXpqtM
UAt555dzZKarSyiO7Iv6fLdlV7ZK3E/tP1Ew1f42RM0v94FkLIW2/irGPSK9w4Eg
aI2XYCKrOv6AFjlLuwt82SpqareG1xXNAOt+CQSG7GdX9vQ044c3uw==
-----END CERTIFICATE-----

Back in cPanel; paste the certificate data into the certificate box. As you do this you'll see information about the certificate under this box:

Paste the certificate into the following text box:
CloudFlare Origin Certificate
Domains: *.harlun.co.uk
harlun.co.uk
Issuer: CloudFlare, Inc.
Key Size: 2,048 bits (a291a99f ...)
Expiration: Mar 18, 2033 12:38:01 PM

As you can see, CloudFlare, Inc. is now the issuer for the certificate on this site. It expires on March 18th, 2033. That's 15 years from now.

In the description box, just enter the domain name.

Click on the **Save Certificate** button.

If everything went to plan you'll get a notification to confirm the certificate saved successfully:

SSL/TLS
The certificate for the domain "CloudFlare Origin Certificate" has been saved.

Activate the certificate

We need to carry out one final step before the domain can use the certificate.

Back in cPanel, scroll down to **SECURITY** and click on the **SSL/TLS** icon.

Click on the final option **Install and Manage SSL for your site (HTTPS).**

Install and Manage SSL for your site (HTTPS)
Manage SSL sites.

Scroll all the way to the bottom to find the **Install an SSL Website** section.

Select your domain from the **Select a Domain** drop-down box:

Browse Certificates
Domain
harlun.co.uk (+ subdomains: cpa
Autofill by Domain

When you select the domain, a new button appears offering to **Autofill by Domain.**

You can click this button if you deleted the old obsolete certificates for your domain. It will find the only certificate on your server for this domain. In other words, the one we installed earlier.

Here's how that looks for my domain:

Certificate: (CRT)
-----BEGIN CERTIFICATE-----
Domains: CloudFlare Origin Certificate
*.harlun.co.uk
harlun.co.uk
Issuer: CloudFlare, Inc.
Key Size: 2,048 bits (a291a99f ...)
Expiration: Mar 18, 2033 12:38:01 PM
The certificate may already be on your server. You can either paste the certificate here or try to retrieve it for your domain.

Bingo! It's the correct certificate.

But what if you didn't delete the old certificates? Well, cPanel will stop when it finds the first valid certificate and try to use that.

In this case, you'll need to manually find the correct certificate. If **Autofill by Domain** didn't work for you, click on the **Browse Certificates** button.

A popup appears showing all the certificates on your server. You can order these by **Expiration** date which makes finding your certificate much easier.

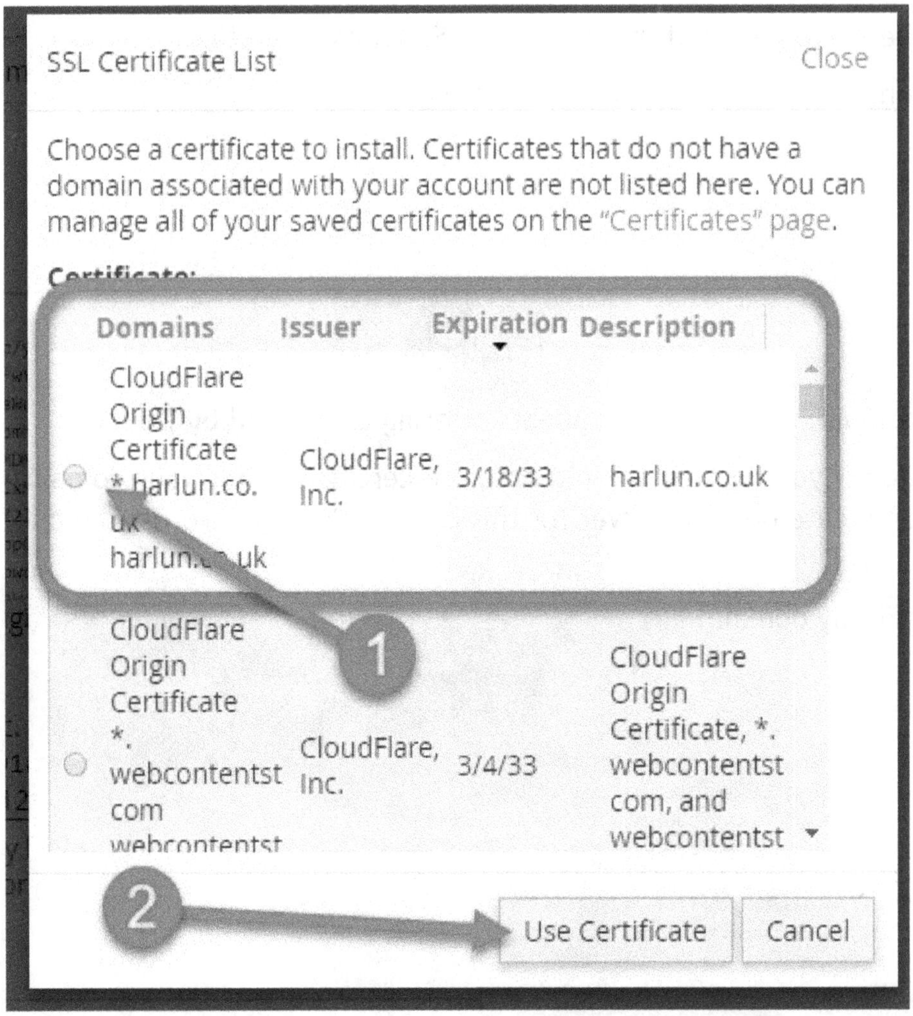
SSL Certificate List
Close
Choose a certificate to install. Certificates that do not have a domain associated with your account are not listed here. You can manage all of your saved certificates on the "Certificates" page.
Domains
Issuer
Expiration
Description
CloudFlare Origin Certificate
CloudFlare, Inc.
3/18/33
harlun.co.uk
CloudFlare Origin Certificate
CloudFlare, Inc.
3/4/33
1
2
Use Certificate
Cancel

Select the correct certificate and then click the **Use Certificate** button.

The information contained in the certificate is used to populate the **Certificate (CRT)**, **Private Key (KEY)** and **Certificate Authority Bundle (CABUNDLE)** boxes. Don't worry if the last box is empty. The system will fetch that information as you install the certificate.

With the correct certificate now ready for installation, click the **Install Certificate** button:

cnRpZmljYXRlIEF1dGhvcml0eTEWMBQGA1UEBxMNU2FuI
A1UECBMKQ2FsaWZvcm5pYTCCASIwDQYJKoZIhvcNAQEBB
AMBIlWf1KEKR5hbB75OYrAcUXobpD/AxvSYRXr91mbRu+
In most cases, you do no need to suppl
because the server wi etch it from a pu
installation.
Install Certificate
Reset

If everything has gone to plan, you should get confirmation that the certificate is now in use for your site:

SSL Host Successfully Installed
You have successfully configured SSL.
The SSL website is now active and accessible via HTTPS on these domains:
harlun.co.uk
mail.harlun.co.uk
The SSL website is also accessible via this domain, but the certificate does not support it. Web browsers will show a warning when accessing this domain via HTTPS:
harlun.cheebles.com
The SSL certificate also supports this domain, but
OK

You can quickly check that everything has gone according to plan. First, close the notification screen. Now scroll down the certificates to find your domain. It should now show the Cloudflare Origin Certificate:

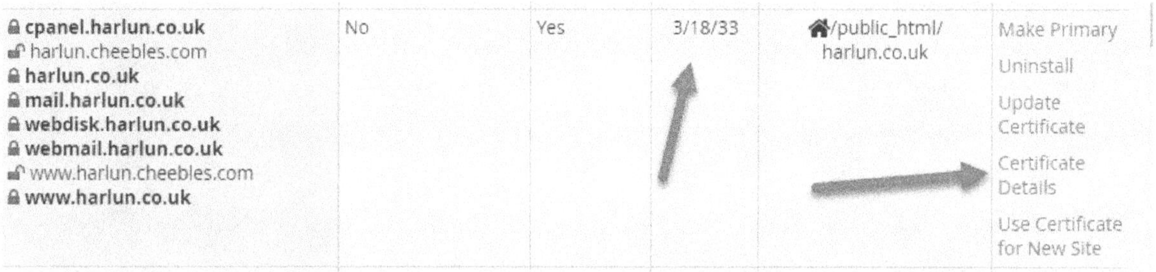
cpanel.harlun.co.uk
harlun.cheebles.com
harlun.co.uk
mail.harlun.co.uk
webdisk.harlun.co.uk
webmail.harlun.co.uk
www.harlun.cheebles.com
www.harlun.co.uk
No
Yes
3/18/33
/public_html/
harlun.co.uk
Make Primary
Uninstall
Update Certificate
Certificate Details
Use Certificate for New Site

As you can see from the screenshot, the certificate for the domain expires in 2033. I can now view the certificate information by clicking the **Certificate Details** link.

Certificate ID: CloudFlare_Origin_Certificate_
Domains: CloudFlare Origin Certificate
*.harlun.co.uk
harlun.co.uk
Issuer: CloudFlare, Inc.
Key Size: 2,048 bits (a291a99f ...)
Expiration: Mar 18, 2033 12:38:01 PM

Here I can see the issuer, expiry date, and other data.

Our site now has an Edge Certificate and an Origin Certificate. Now we can switch over to Full (strict) SSL.

SECTION 3 - For Everyone

At this point, everyone should be in the same position. You have an **Origin Certificate** (either from Cloudflare or AutoSSL) and an **Edge Certificate** from Cloudflare.

With the two certificates installed, we need to switch the SSL to Full (strict) and check that everything works as it should.

That's what this section of the book covers.

Switch to Full (strict)

Login to Cloudflare and head for the **Crypto** section.

Change the SSL to **Full (strict)**. You don't need to save the changes as they save automatically.

If you now head to your website, you can check whether the HTTPS version is working properly. You should now see the green padlock and **Secure** message.

Here is mine:

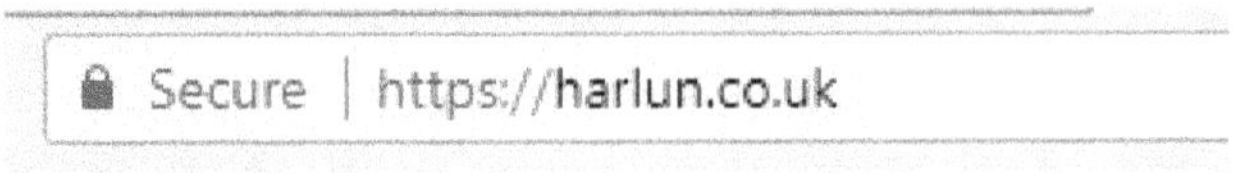
Secure | https://harlun.co.uk

That's great as it means everything is working as it should. However, when you first switch a site over you will get a slightly different message that looks like this:

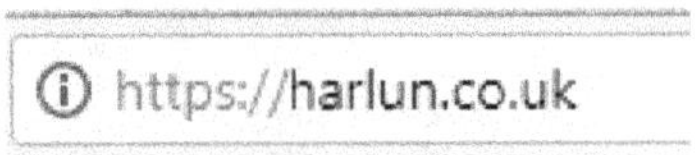
https://harlun.co.uk

The HTTPS version of the web page loads OK but you don't get the padlock and Secure message.

We'll look at why this happens and how to fix it later in the book. For now, let's continue with the conversion. As things stand, we probably still have HTTP AND HTTPs versions of our site available.

Secure the Dashboard

In this chapter, we're going to make sure the WordPress Dashboard for our site automatically goes in through a secure HTTPS connection.

Login to your site's Dashboard through your normal HTTP connection.

Once logged in, change the HTTP to HTTPs in the address bar of your browser. Now press the return key to load the secure version.

The system might log you out when you do this. If it does, just log back in again.

If the Dashboard loads fine with the HTTPs, you can be fairly sure that everything's working properly. What we need to do next is force your Dashboard to always log in via the secure HTTPs version.

To do this we need to edit the wp-config.php file of our WordPress site.

Login to cPanel and start the FileManager:

FILES
File Manager

Navigate to the root folder of your website and look for the wp-config.php file. Click the file to select it and then click the Edit button at the top of the FileManager screen:

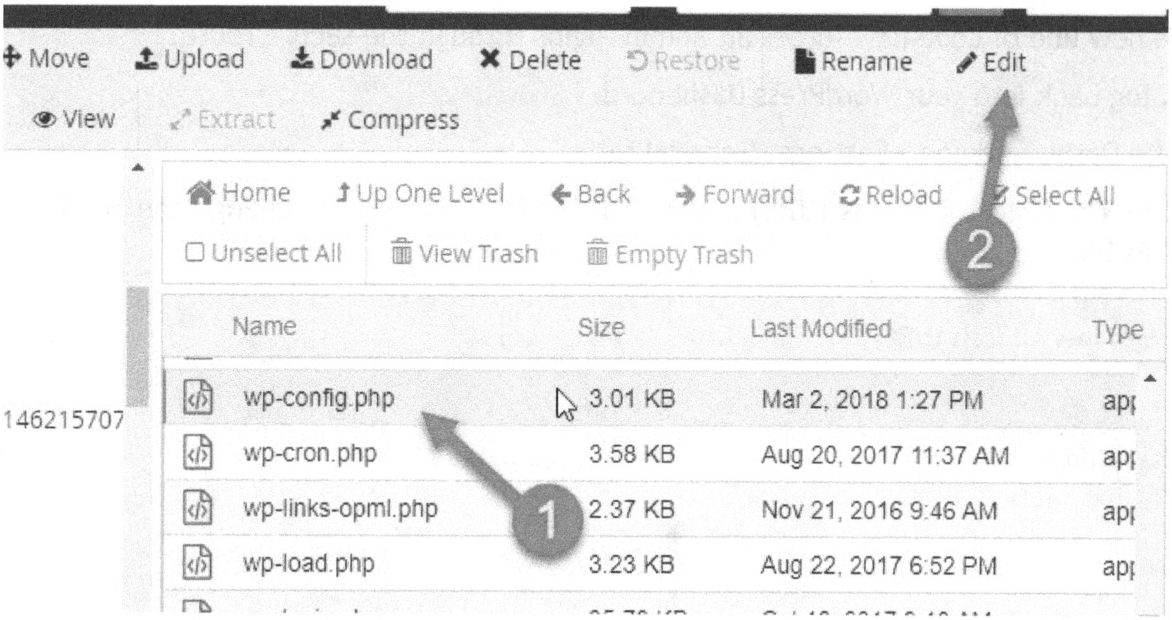
Move
Upload
Download
Delete
Restore
Rename
Edit
View
Extract
Compress
Home
Up One Level
Back
Forward
Reload
Select All
Unselect All
View Trash
Empty Trash
2
Name
Size
Last Modified
Type
146215707
wp-config.php
3.01 KB
Mar 2, 2018 1:27 PM
wp-cron.php
3.58 KB
Aug 20, 2017 11:37 AM
wp-links-opml.php
2.37 KB
Nov 21, 2016 9:46 AM
wp-load.php
3.23 KB
Aug 22, 2017 6:52 PM
1

The file will open in a text editor.

Scroll to the bottom of the file and look for this line:

```
 */
define('WP_DEBUG', false);

/* That's all, stop editing! Happy blogging. */

/** Absolute path to the WordPress directory. */
if ( !defined('ABSPATH') )
    define('ABSPATH', dirname(__FILE__) . '/');

/** Sets up WordPress vars and included files. */
require_once(ABSPATH . 'wp-settings.php');
```

Position your cursor at the end of the line and press the return key a couple of times to insert two lines below.

Now insert this line of code:

define('FORCE_SSL_ADMIN', true);

Your file should now look like this:

```

/* That's all, stop editing! Happy blogging. */

define('FORCE_SSL_ADMIN', true);

/** Absolute path to the WordPress directory. */
if ( !defined('ABSPATH') )
    define('ABSPATH', dirname(__FILE__) . '/');
```

At the top of the editor, click the **Save Changes** button and then the **Close** button to close the text editor.

This new line of code now forces all admin logins through the secure route.

OK, log back into your WordPress Dashboard.

In the Dashboard go to **Settings, General** tab.

In the **WordPress Address (URL)** and **Site Address (URL)** boxes, change the HTTP to HTTPs like so.

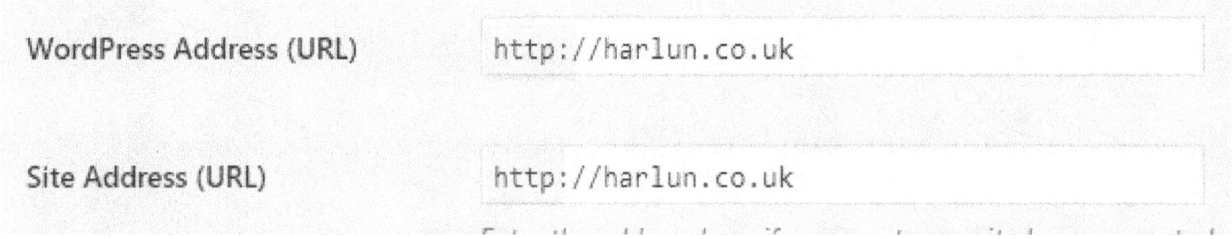
WordPress Address (URL)
http://harlun.co.uk
Site Address (URL)
http://harlun.co.uk

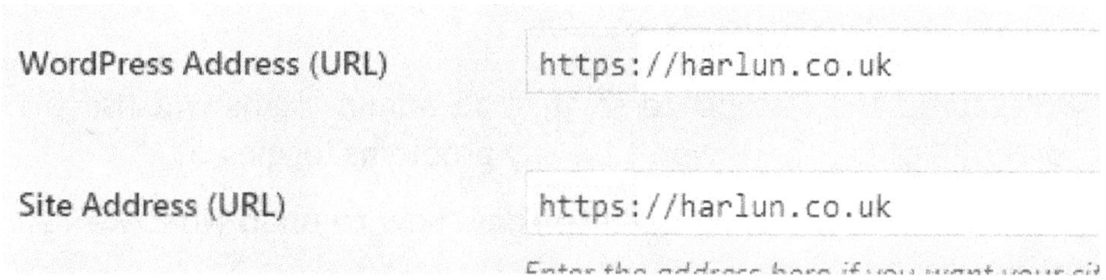
WordPress Address (URL)
https://harlun.co.uk
Site Address (URL)
https://harlun.co.uk

Don't change anything else about these URLs, just the HTTP prefix.

Now scroll to the bottom and click **Save Changes**.

Congratulations, you have just secured your Dashboard. Now every time you log in you'll always go in via the secure HTTPS route.

Check the next chapter if you have problems trying to log in. It shows you what to do if WordPress locks you out.

If you get locked out of the Dashboard

In the last chapter, we secured the Dashboard so that all admin logins will use the secure HTTPS route. For 99.9% of us, there won't be any problems logging in.

Problems can arise for some, though, so you need to know how to undo what we just did in case you have issues at some point.

To give you an example, I accidentally edited a URL when I upgraded one of my own sites to HTTPS. Here's a screenshot of what I did:

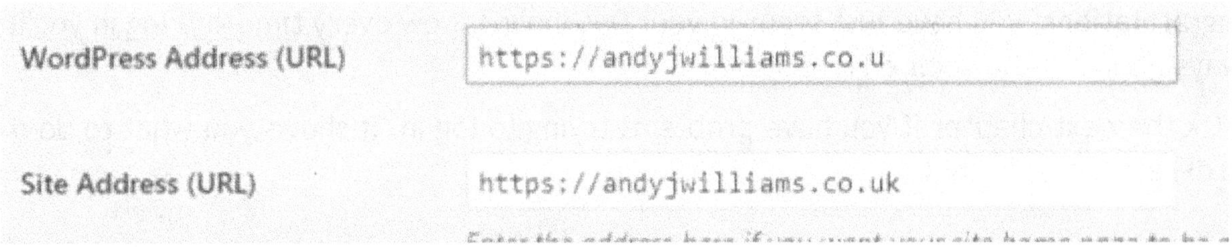

WordPress Address (URL)
https://andyjwilliams.co.u
Site Address (URL)
https://andyjwilliams.co.uk

Can you see my error?

I accidentally deleted the **k** from the end of the **WordPress Address (URL)**. That meant I couldn't log back into the dashboard. This is because the URL that WordPress thought should be there didn't exist.

The good news is that there are ways to fix issues if you can't log back into the Dashboard. This chapter shows you how.

You need access to the WordPress files on your server. I will use File Manager inside cPanel to access mine.

The file we need to edit is your functions.php which is in your themes folder. And the 'themes' folder is located inside the **wp-content** folder:

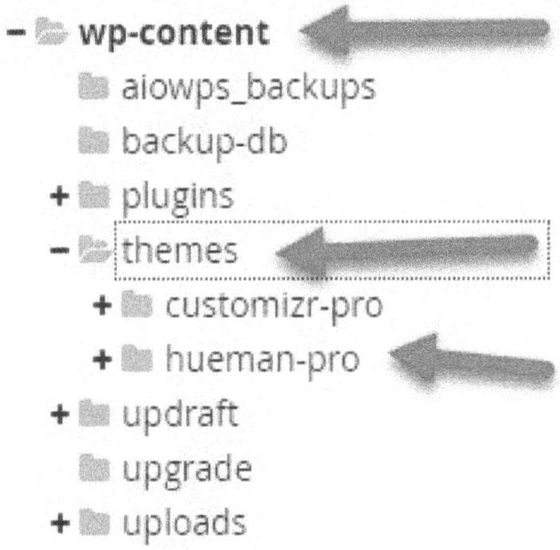

wp-content
aiowps_backups
backup-db
plugins
themes
customizr-pro
hueman-pro
updraft
upgrade
uploads

All your installed themes are located in the **themes** subfolder. **Click** it **to** open.

I have two themes installed in my screenshot, Customizr-Pro and Hueman-Pro. The one my site uses is the second one so I need to open that folder:

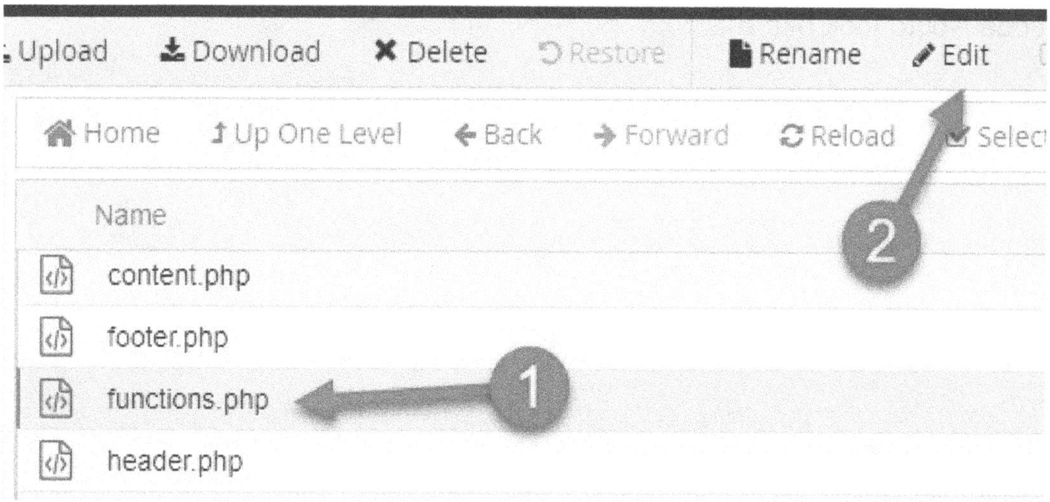
Upload
Download
Delete
Restore
Rename
Edit
Home
Up One Level
Back
Forward
Reload
Selec
2
Name
content.php
footer.php
functions.php
1
header.php

Inside you will find the functions.php file. Click to select it, and then click on the **Edit** button to open the file in a text editor:

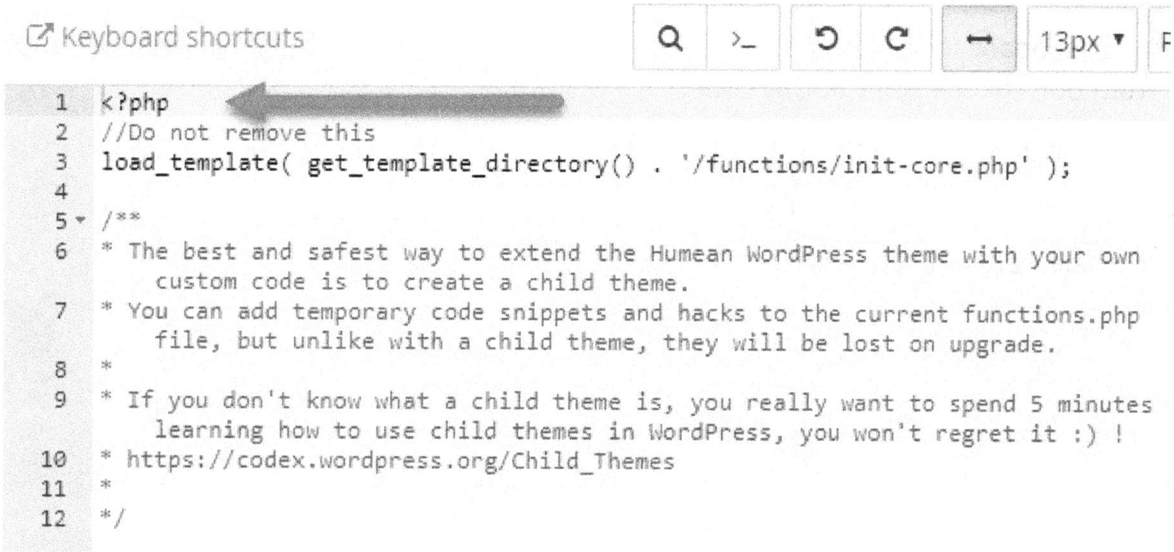
Keyboard shortcuts
13px
<?php
//Do not remove this
load_template(get_template_directory() . '/functions/init-core.php');
/**
* The best and safest way to extend the Humean WordPress theme with your own custom code is to create a child theme.
* You can add temporary code snippets and hacks to the current functions.php file, but unlike with a child theme, they will be lost on upgrade.
*
* If you don't know what a child theme is, you really want to spend 5 minutes learning how to use child themes in WordPress, you won't regret it :) !
* https://codex.wordpress.org/Child_Themes
*
*/

Your functions.php file will look different to mine but the first line will be the same. Position your cursor at the end of the first line, right after the **<?php**.

Press the return key a couple of times to insert two blank lines.

We're now going to add some code to this file. This code updates two of the options inside the Dashboard for us as we log in.

Here it is:

update_option('siteurl', http://example.com');

update_option('home', 'http://example.com');

You need to edit this so that your correct WordPress Address and Site Address replace the example.com site in the above code.

For me, my code would look like this:

```
<?php

update_option( 'siteurl', 'https://andyjwilliams.co.uk' );
update_option( 'home', 'https://andyjwilliams.co.uk' );

//Do not remove this
load_template( get_template_directory() . '/functions/init-core.php' );

/**
 * The best and safest way to extend the Humean WordPress theme with your own custom code is to create a child theme.
 * You can add temporary code snippets and hacks to the current functions.php file, but unlike with a child theme, they will be lost on upgrade.
 *
```

Now when I go to login to the Dashboard, the **WordPress Address (URL)** in the Dashboard (that had accidentally lost the final **k)** will be overwritten to the correct URL.

If your Dashboard locks you out because of the forced secure login, simply remove the “s” from both of the URLs in this code.

Save the file once you've done that.

You can now log back into your Dashboard.

Head to the **Settings**, **General** tab.

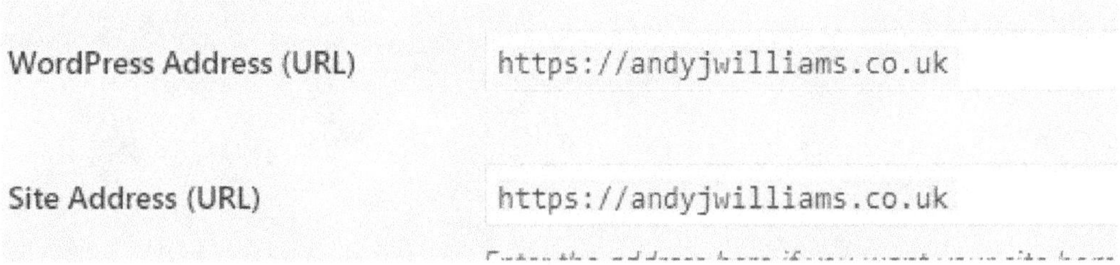
WordPress Address (URL)
https://andyjwilliams.co.uk
Site Address (URL)
https://andyjwilliams.co.uk

You will see that the values in **WordPress Address** and **Site Address** have been over-written. They're now the same as the URLs we added to the functions.php file.

Immediately scroll to the bottom of the page and save the settings.

This will save the settings in Dashboard so you no longer need those lines in the functions.php file.

Go back to your cPanel and open the functions.php file again. Now remove those two lines and save the changes.

Redirect HTTP to HTTPs

Adding an SSL certificate and making a secure HTTPS version doesn't remove the insecure HTTP version of a site. That's not great for the reasons mentioned earlier.

We need to make sure that all connections are forced to use the secure HTTPS connection. We can do that by simply redirecting any HTTP requests so that they go through the HTTPS version of the page instead. We'll create this redirect in the site's .htaccess file.

If you use a caching plugin on your site you need to do a couple of things before you create these redirects.

Go in and:

a) Purge the entire cache.
b) Disable the cache.

You can re-enable it again after you have completed this chapter.

OK, ready to add the redirects?

Login to cPanel and open File Manager so you can see your site's root directory.

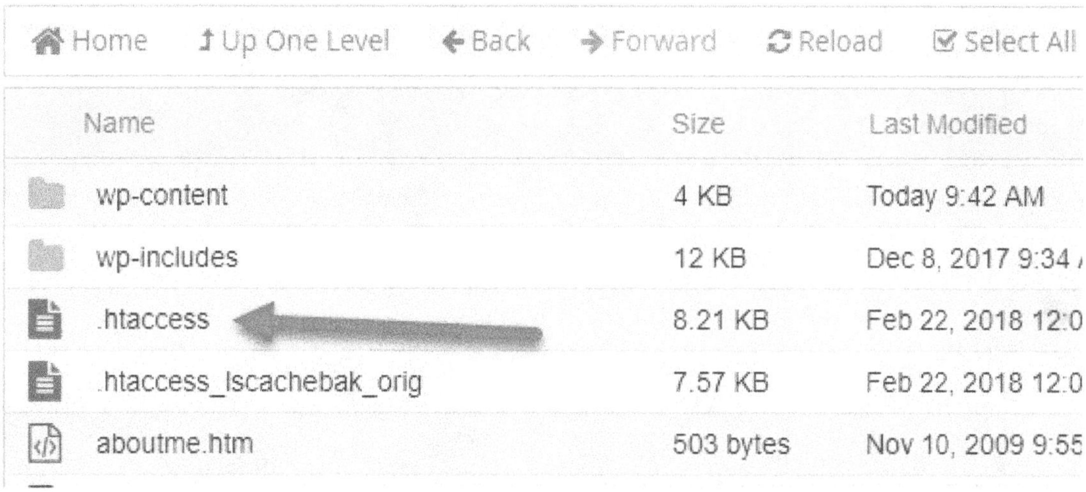
Home
Up One Level
Back
Forward
Reload
Select All
Name
Size
Last Modified
wp-content
4 KB
Today 9:42 AM
wp-includes
12 KB
Dec 8, 2017 9:34
.htaccess
8.21 KB
Feb 22, 2018 12:0
.htaccess_lscachebak_orig
7.57 KB
Feb 22, 2018 12:0
aboutme.htm
503 bytes
Nov 10, 2009 9:55

You should see the .htaccess file in the root folder. If you don't, chances are it's a hidden file. To unhide this file, click the **Settings** button located at the top right of File Manager.

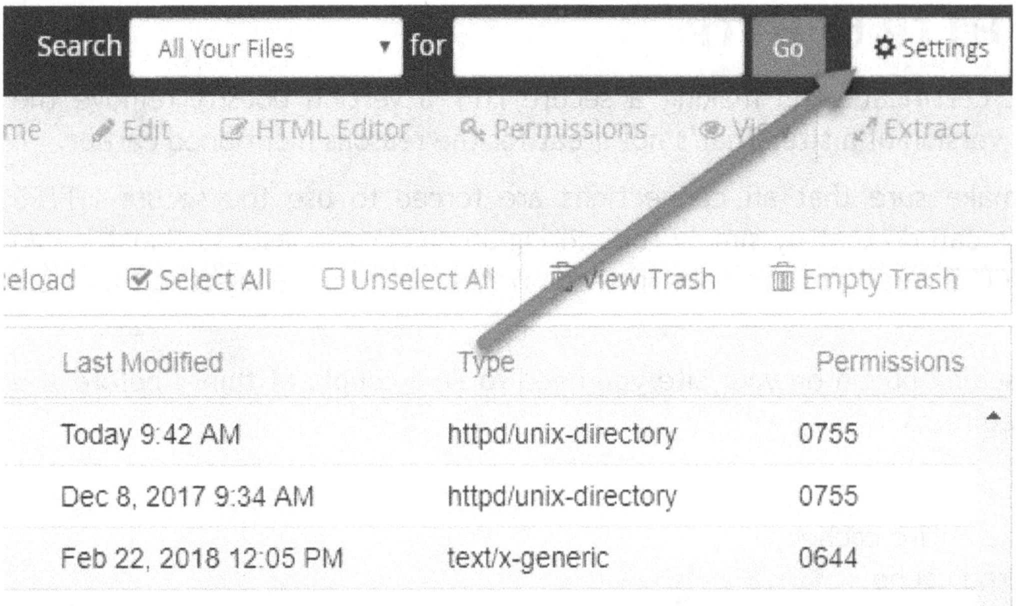
Search
All Your Files
for
Go
Settings
Edit
HTML Editor
Permissions
Extract
Select All
Unselect All
View Trash
Empty Trash
Last Modified
Type
Permissions
Today 9:42 AM
httpd/unix-directory
0755
Dec 8, 2017 9:34 AM
httpd/unix-directory
0755
Feb 22, 2018 12:05 PM
text/x-generic
0644

You will see an option at the bottom of the **Settings** screen to **Show Hidden Files.**

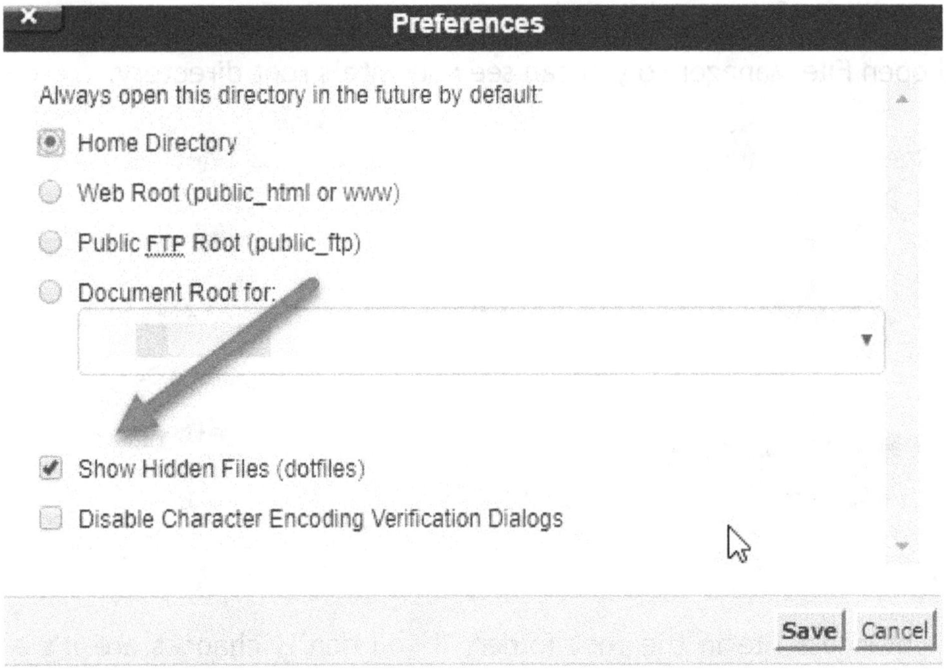
Preferences
Always open this directory in the future by default:
Home Directory
Web Root (public_html or www)
Public FTP Root (public_ftp)
Document Root for:
Show Hidden Files (dotfiles)
Disable Character Encoding Verification Dialogs
Save
Cancel

Make sure it's checked and then click the **Save** button. Your .htaccess should now be visible in File Manager.

Click to select the file and then click the **Edit** button.

Scroll down the file until you come to a comment that says **# BEGIN WordPress:**

```
# BEGIN WordPress
<IfModule mod_rewrite.c>
RewriteEngine On
RewriteBase /
RewriteRule ^index\.php$ - [L]
RewriteCond %{REQUEST_FILENAME} !-f
RewriteCond %{REQUEST_FILENAME} !-d
RewriteRule . /index.php [L]
</IfModule>

# END WordPress

```

Move your mouse cursor to the end of the line that says **RewriteEngine On.** Now press the return key a couple of times to insert two blank lines. We now need to insert this code:

RewriteCond %{HTTPS} off

RewriteRule ^(.*)$ HTTPs://%{HTTP_HOST}%{REQUEST_URI} [L,R=301]

Here is my .htaccess file after adding those lines:

```
# BEGIN WordPress
<IfModule mod_rewrite.c>
RewriteEngine On
RewriteCond %{HTTPS} off
RewriteRule ^(.*)$ https://%{HTTP_HOST}%{REQUEST_URI} [L,R=301]
RewriteBase /
RewriteRule ^index\.php$ - [L]
RewriteCond %{REQUEST_FILENAME} !-f
RewriteCond %{REQUEST_FILENAME} !-d
RewriteRule . /index.php [L]
</IfModule>
```

Essentially, if anyone or anything tries to access an HTTP version of something, this code will redirect them to the HTTPs version of the same URL.

We have now completed the main work in securing our website. All we need to do is check everything works as expected and that we have the **padlock** and **Secure** message.

Check your SSL

Load your website and open a few pages. They should all load using the HTTPS version. You should also see the padlock and **Secure** message but don't worry if not. The reason is something called insecure or **Mixed Content**.

What is mixed content?

Mixed content is when a secure HTTPS webpage loads something (e.g., an image) through an insecure HTTP link.

Some data transmits to and from web pages via insecure, unencrypted links. In these instances, you won't have the padlock and the **Secure** message.

Here' an example from my own site:

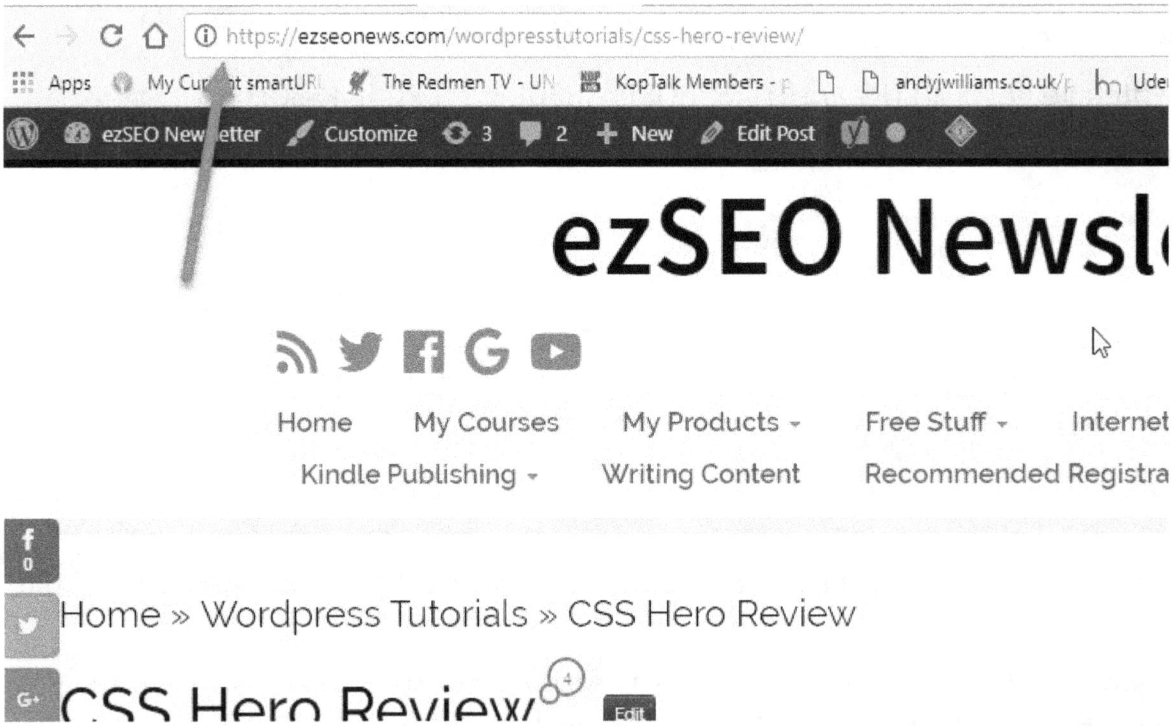
https://ezseonews.com/wordpresstutorials/css-hero-review/
Apps
The Redmen TV - UN
KopTalk Members -
andyjwilliams.co.uk/
Customize
New
Edit Post
ezSEO Newsl
Home
My Courses
My Products
Free Stuff
Internet
Kindle Publishing
Writing Content
Recommended Registra
Home » Wordpress Tutorials » CSS Hero Review

As you can see, the webpage loads with the HTTPS but I don't have the padlock. Instead, I have a circle with an "i" inside, which stands for information. Clicking the "i" gives you more information:

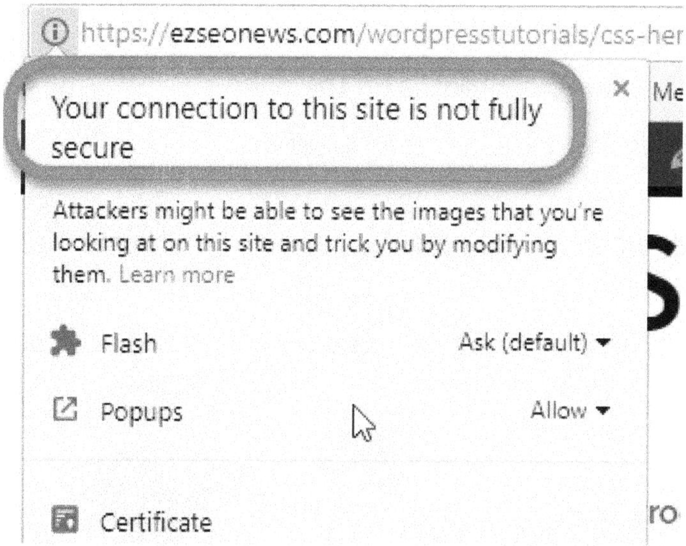
https://ezseonews.com/wordpresstutorials/css-her
Your connection to this site is not fully secure
Attackers might be able to see the images that you're looking at on this site and trick you by modifying them. Learn more
Flash
Ask (default)
Popups
Allow
Certificate

That screenshot is in Google Chrome. Here's the same page loaded in Firefox:

https://ezseonews.com/wordpresstutorials/css-hero-review/
ezSEO News

This web browser shows a warning triangle. Clicking the triangle gives you more information:

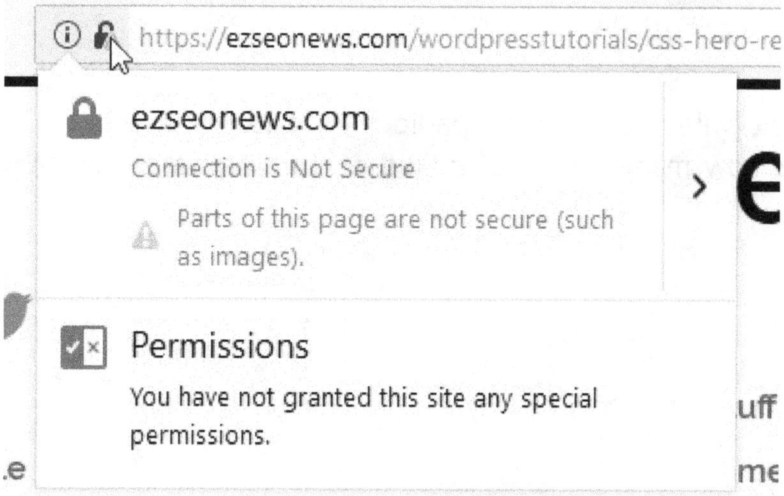
https://ezseonews.com/wordpresstutorials/css-hero-re
ezseonews.com
Connection is Not Secure
Parts of this page are not secure (such as images).
Permissions
You have not granted this site any special permissions.

This is something we obviously need to fix.

Fixing mixed content

The first thing to do is find out where the mixed content is on the page.

We're going to use a Chrome browser plugin as well as a free web service to help identify mixed content.

You must have Google Chrome installed to continue. Now head over to the Chrome Web Store (search Google if you need to).

Search for **HTTPs mixed content locator** in the store's search box. This is the one you want to **Add to Chrome**:

HTTPS Mixed Content Locator
offered by https://www.pericror.com
Easily locate and identify mixed content on any HTTPS site.
RATE IT
Developer Tools
(4)

I already have it installed on my machine. Once installed and active you'll see a new icon in the Chrome toolbar.

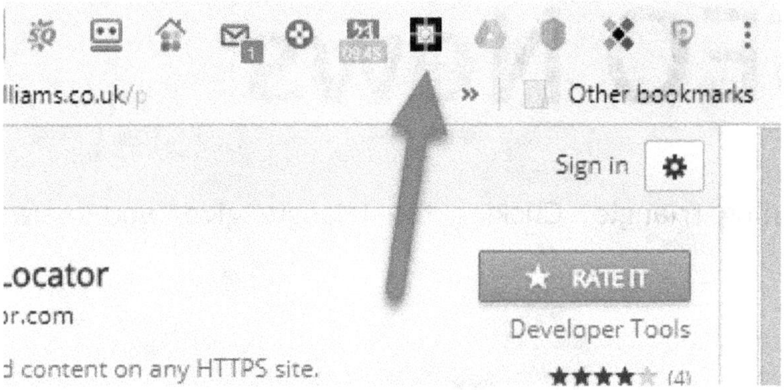
Other bookmarks
Sign in
RATE IT
Developer Tools

Now visit one of your pages that failed to show the padlock. The icon will contain a number. This number indicates how many pieces of mixed content there are on the page. It found seven on mine:

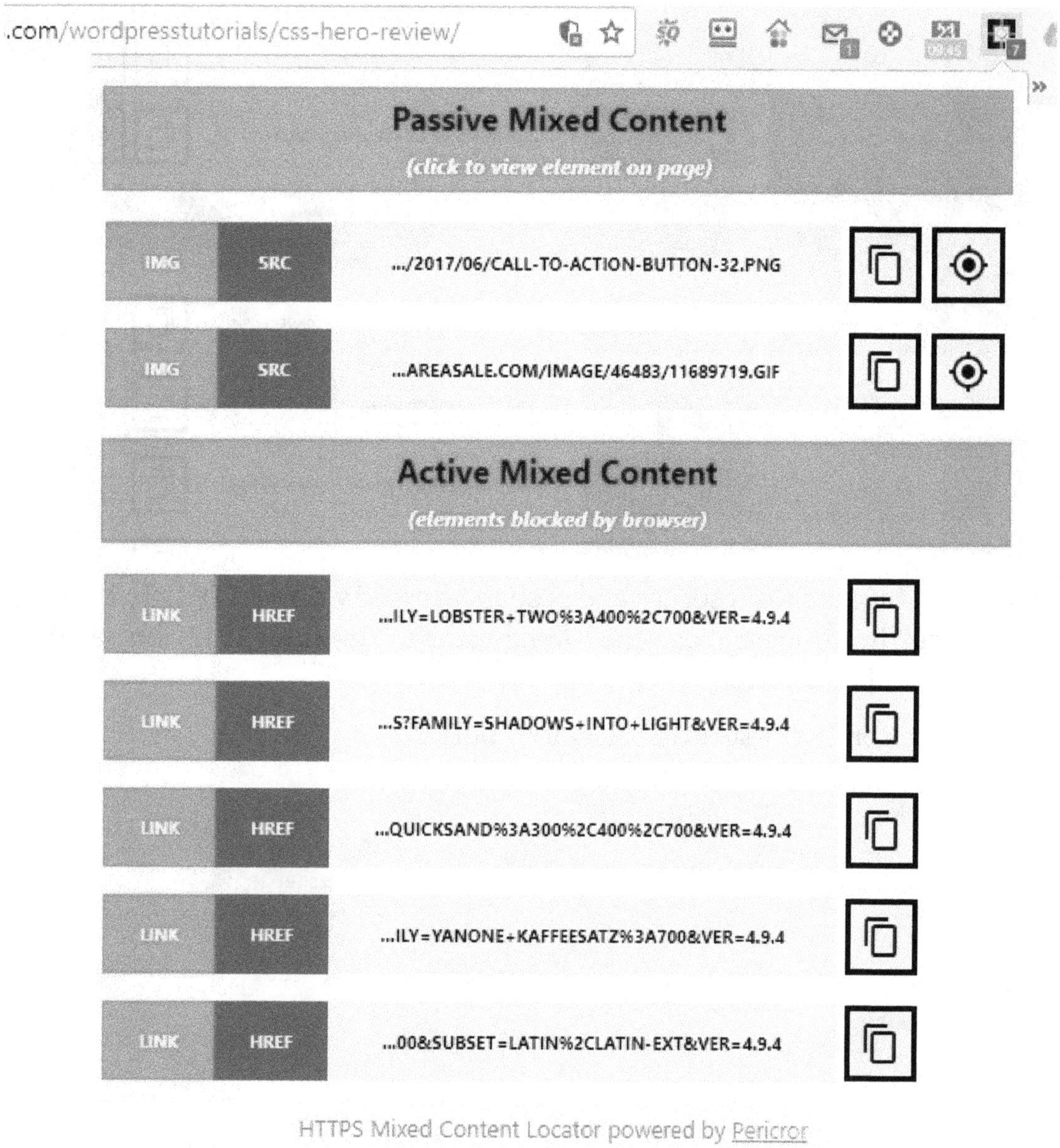
.com/wordpresstutorials/css-hero-review/
Passive Mixed Content
(click to view element on page)
IMG
SRC
.../2017/06/CALL-TO-ACTION-BUTTON-32.PNG
IMG
SRC
...AREASALE.COM/IMAGE/46483/11689719.GIF
Active Mixed Content
(elements blocked by browser)
LINK
HREF
...ILY=LOBSTER+TWO%3A400%2C700&VER=4.9.4
LINK
HREF
...S?FAMILY=SHADOWS+INTO+LIGHT&VER=4.9.4
LINK
HREF
...QUICKSAND%3A300%2C400%2C700&VER=4.9.4
LINK
HREF
...ILY=YANONE+KAFFEESATZ%3A700&VER=4.9.4
LINK
HREF
...00&SUBSET=LATIN%2CLATIN-EXT&VER=4.9.4
HTTPS Mixed Content Locator powered by Pericror

HTTPs mixed content locator splits these seven issues into two groups. The first is **Passive Mixed Content** which is still on the web page. When I click the bull's-eye button next to this content it highlights the offending code on the page. For example, if I click on the button for the first item it highlights the offending image on that page:

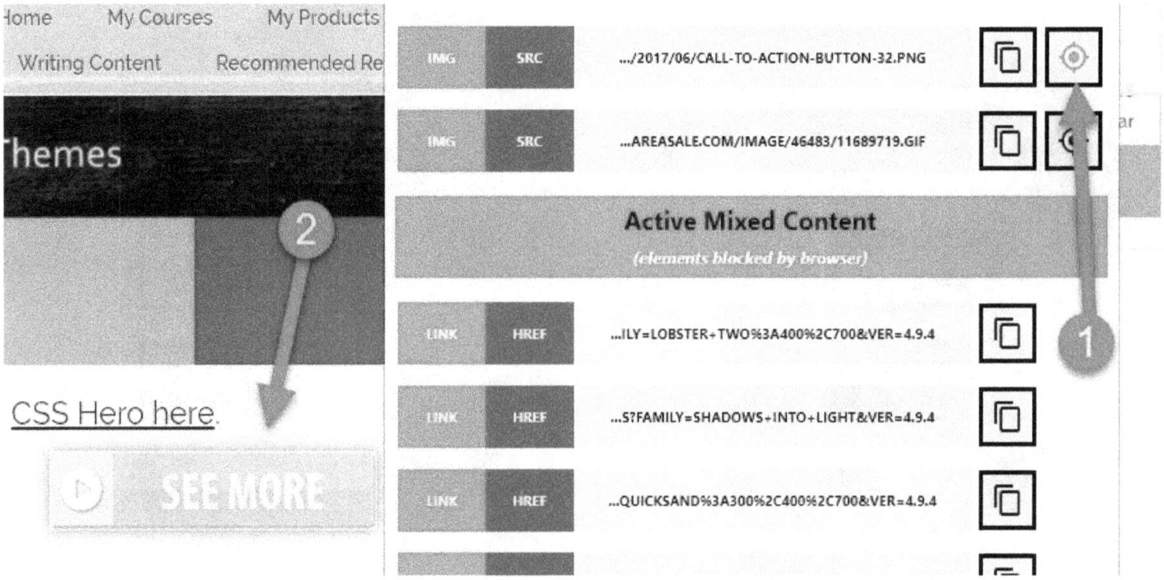
Home
My Courses
My Products
Writing Content
Recommended Re
Themes
2
CSS Hero here.
SEE MORE
IMG
SRC
.../2017/06/CALL-TO-ACTION-BUTTON-32.PNG
...AREASALE.COM/IMAGE/46483/11689719.GIF
Active Mixed Content
(elements blocked by browser)
LINK
HREF
...ILY=LOBSTER+TWO%3A400%2C700&VER=4.9.4
...S?FAMILY=SHADOWS+INTO+LIGHT&VER=4.9.4
...QUICKSAND%3A300%2C400%2C700&VER=4.9.4
1

I now know that this image is insecure and probably served via an HTTP link. I can check this in Chrome by bringing up the webmaster's **Console** (F12 on a PC, or Command+Option+J on a Mac).

Once loaded, click on the first little "selector" button:

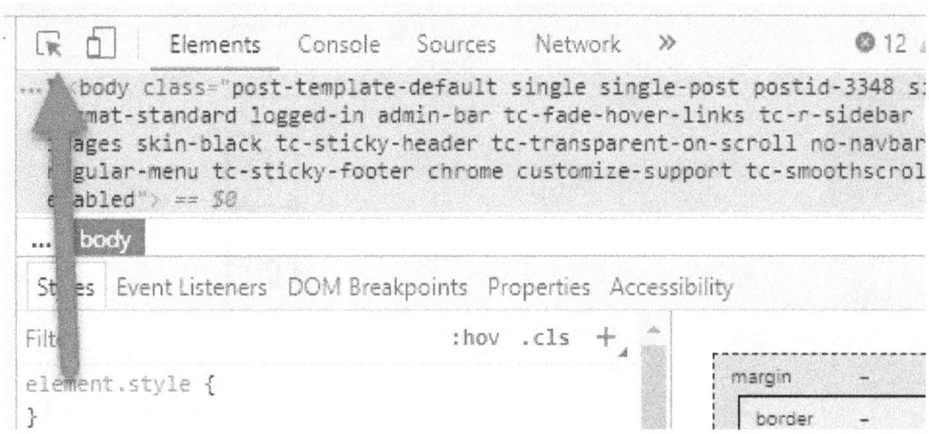
Elements
Console
Sources
Network
12
body
Event Listeners
DOM Breakpoints
Properties
Accessibility
:hov .cls +
margin
border

Then click on the insecure element. The code for that element will appear in the console. Here it is for that image:

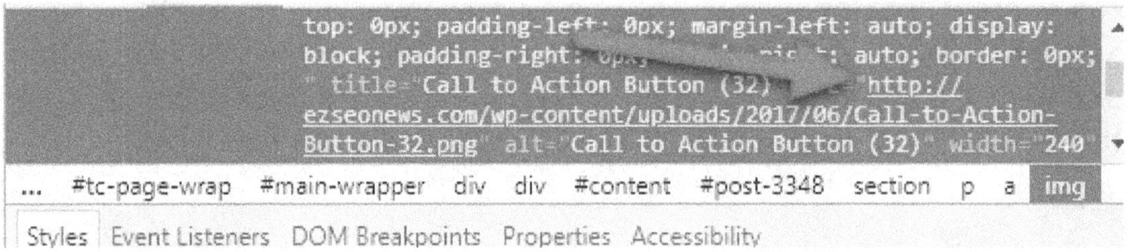
top: 0px; padding-left: 0px; margin-left: auto; display:
block; padding-right:
auto; border: 0px;
title="Call to Action Button (32)"
"http://
ezseonews.com/wp-content/uploads/2017/06/Call-to-Action-
Button-32.png" alt="Call to Action Button (32)" width="240"
... #tc-page-wrap #main-wrapper div div #content #post-3348 section p a img
Styles Event Listeners DOM Breakpoints Properties Accessibility

You can clearly see that the button is called through an insecure HTTP link. I can fix this by editing the source code for the page so that the image loads via HTTPS instead.

You will eventually get the padlock by going through each insecure element and fixing it.

Some sites will have a lot of issues with insecure content. You should be able to fix most of them but there may be some you can't.

We can see an example of this on my site. A plugin I installed added these five pieces of **Active Mixed Content**:

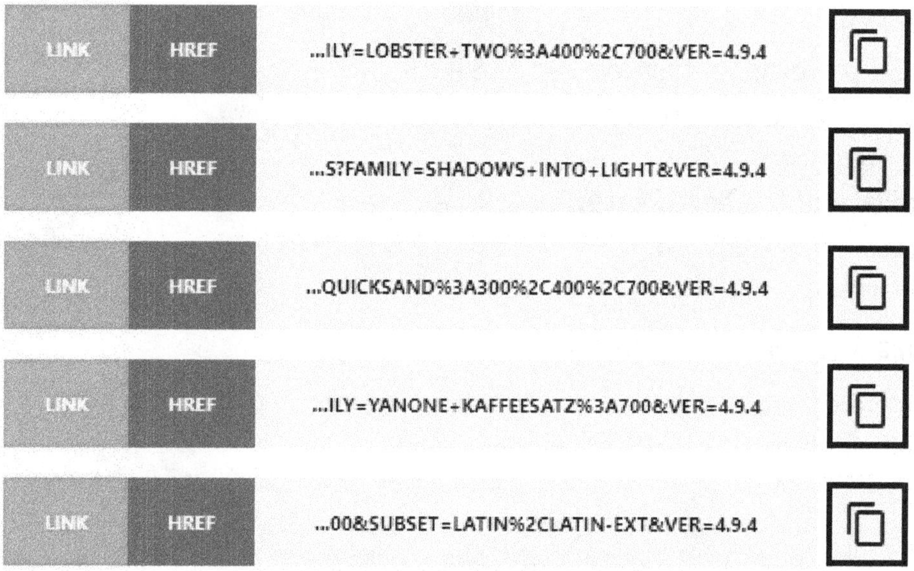
LINK
HREF
...ILY=LOBSTER+TWO%3A400%2C700&VER=4.9.4
LINK
HREF
...S?FAMILY=SHADOWS+INTO+LIGHT&VER=4.9.4
LINK
HREF
...QUICKSAND%3A300%2C400%2C700&VER=4.9.4
LINK
HREF
...ILY=YANONE+KAFFEESATZ%3A700&VER=4.9.4
LINK
HREF
...00&SUBSET=LATIN%2CLATIN-EXT&VER=4.9.4

The problem with this particular plugin is that no one updates it anymore. That means the author hasn't changed the references in the code to use a secure connection. Unless I have access to the source code of the plugin (and know how to code), I can't fix this mixed content by myself.

I could just remove the plugin and find an alternative. In this particular case, though, there are no alternatives for what this plugin does—and I want to keep it.

The good news is we have a solution. There's a WordPress plugin that can fix this for us—on the fly. We'll take a look at that later.

If you have mixed content you can fix, like the first image I showed you, then you should fix it using that method.

Occasionally you will find some mixed content that's on another website, and that website's not secure. An example would be a Javascript or CSS file downloaded from elsewhere.

In these cases, if you can move that resource to your own server you can serve it from your own HTTPS website. That will secure the content for you. If you cannot move the mixed content and host it yourself you have two other choices. You can either remove it from your site or rely on the plugin we'll look at later.

I want to mention a couple of great resources that can help you find mixed content on your site:

Resource #1 - https://www.whynopadlock.com/

This website allows you to enter a URL to check for SSL and mixed content. I can get a lot of information by running my page through that tool.

Here's what it tells me:

- The certificate issuer.
- Whether my web server is forcing the use of SSL.
- Whether the SSL is installed correctly.
- The certificate signature.
- The expiration date of the certificate.
- The protocol used for protection.
- Mixed Content errors!

That last item provides a list of mixed content issues.

Here's a snapshot of my webpage:

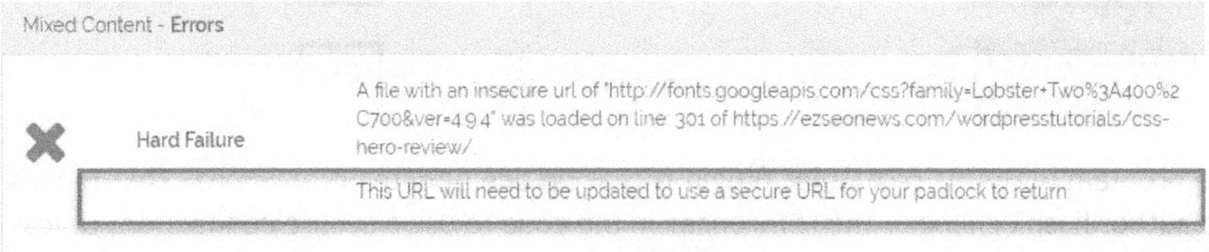
Mixed Content - Errors
Hard Failure
A file with an insecure url of "http://fonts.googleapis.com/css?family=Lobster+Two%3A400%2
C700&ver=4.9.4" was loaded on line: 301 of https://ezseonews.com/wordpresstutorials/css-
hero-review/.
This URL will need to be updated to use a secure URL for your padlock to return.

I get the reason for the failure. Here, it's a resource loaded through an HTTP link. I also get a way to fix it. It suggests updating the URL so it's using a secure HTTPS connection. We've already discussed that. In this case I cannot do this since the code is inside a plugin.

However, the final two messages are the **Passive Mixed Content** we saw earlier:

An image with an insecure url of "http://ezseonews.com/wp-content/uploads/2017/06/Cal
l-to-Action-Button-32.png" was loaded on line: 654 of https://ezseonews.com/wordpresstut
orials/css-hero-review/.
This URL will need to be updated to use a secure URL for your padlock to return.
An image with an insecure url of "http://static.shareasale.com/image/46483/11689719.gif" w
as loaded on line: 784 of https://ezseonews.com/wordpresstutorials/css-hero-review/.
This URL will need to be updated to use a secure URL for your padlock to return.

Both of these images are "fixable".

The first one is an image on my own site so I can probably just change the URL from HTTP to HTTPS.

The second problem is with an image served from the Shareasale website. This will be an affiliate banner so I have two options here. The first is to change the HTTP to HTTPS and see if the image still loads. It should work since Shareasale are secure now. However, I could still easily fix it if there was a problem displaying the image after changing it to HTTPS. I could simply host that image on my own server and use that instead of the one on the Shareasale site.

As it turns out, changing the HTTP to HTTPS for the Shareasale image worked fine. After fixing those two pieces of mixed content I still have five remaining:

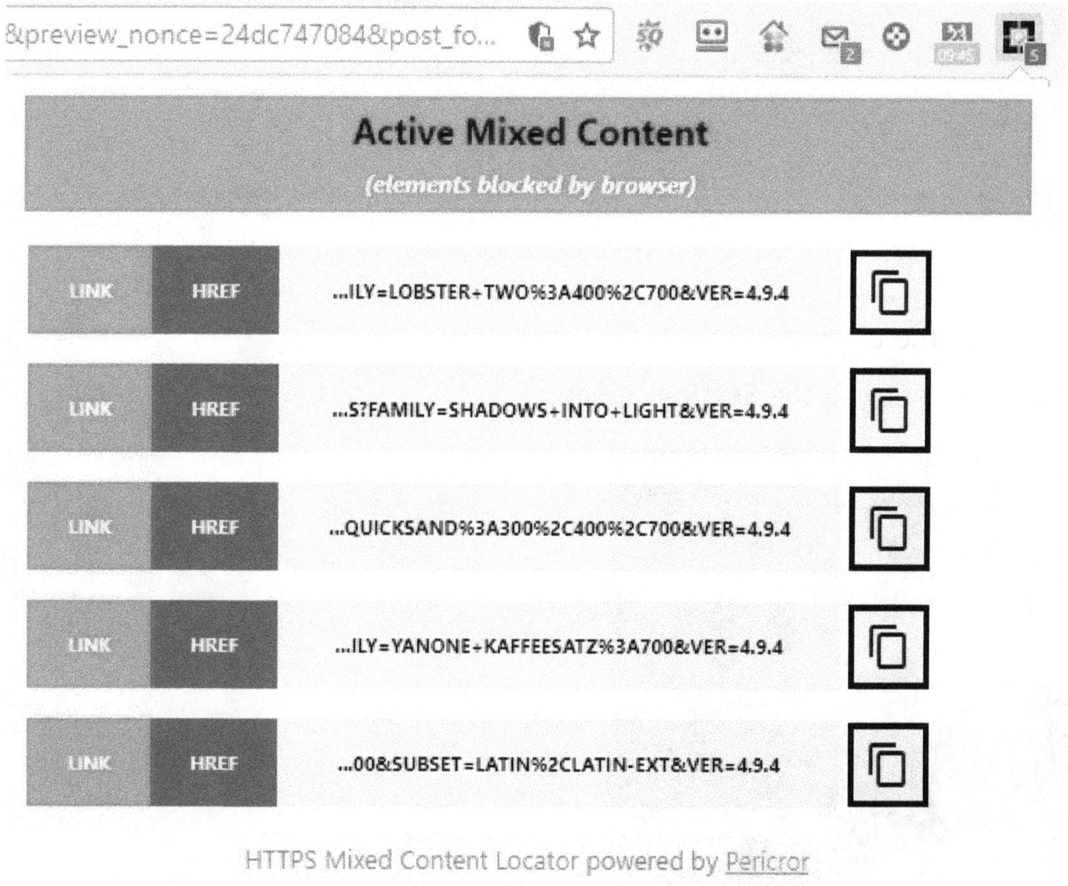
&preview_nonce=24dc747084&post_fo...
Active Mixed Content
(elements blocked by browser)
LINK
HREF
...ILY=LOBSTER+TWO%3A400%2C700&VER=4.9.4
LINK
HREF
...S?FAMILY=SHADOWS+INTO+LIGHT&VER=4.9.4
LINK
HREF
...QUICKSAND%3A300%2C400%2C700&VER=4.9.4
LINK
HREF
...ILY=YANONE+KAFFEESATZ%3A700&VER=4.9.4
LINK
HREF
...00&SUBSET=LATIN%2CLATIN-EXT&VER=4.9.4
HTTPS Mixed Content Locator powered by Pericror

These are the five issues related to the plugin that I cannot fix myself.

The solution for this is in the next chapter.

Insecure Content Plugin

I really recommend you try to fix all the mixed content you can. Use the method outlined in this chapter if, and only if, you still have some unfixable issues.

Login to your WordPress Dashboard and go to **Plugins**, **Add New**.

Search for SSL Insecure Content Fixer.

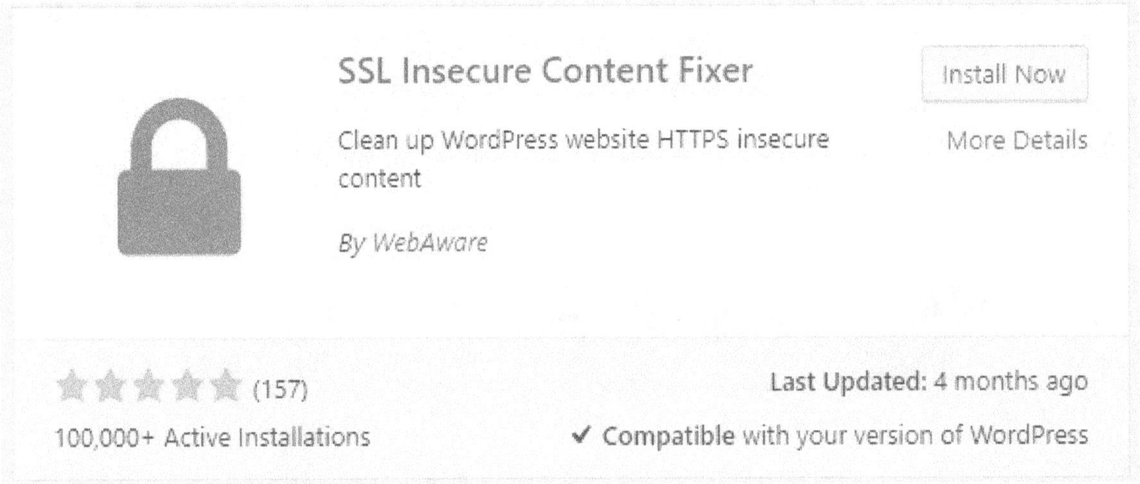
SSL Insecure Content Fixer
Install Now
Clean up WordPress website HTTPS insecure content
More Details
By WebAware
(157)
Last Updated: 4 months ago
100,000+ Active Installations
✓ Compatible with your version of WordPress

Install and activate the plugin.

You will have a new entry in the **Settings** menu:

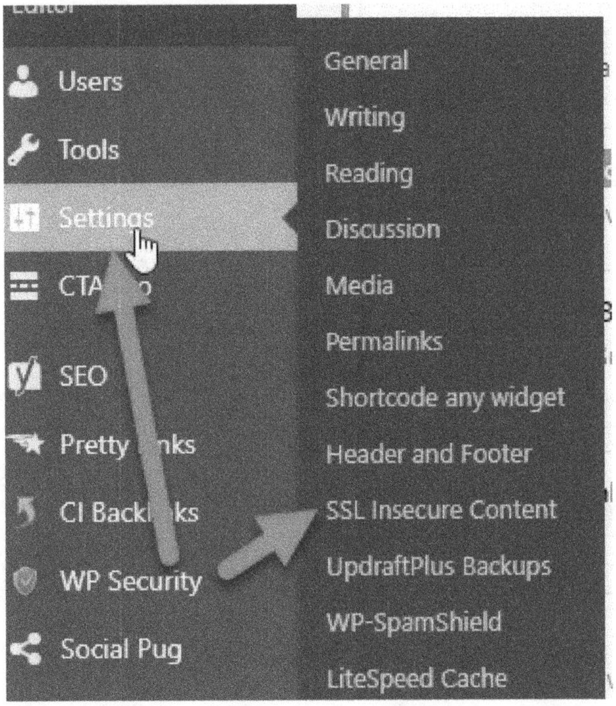
Users
Tools
Settings
SEO
WP Security
Social Pug
General
Writing
Reading
Discussion
Media
Permalinks
Shortcode any widget
Header and Footer
SSL Insecure Content
UpdraftPlus Backups
WP-SpamShield
LiteSpeed Cache

Click on **SSL Insecure Content** to go to the options screen.

I'm not going to go into too much detail with this plugin. Essentially there are different levels of “fixing” available.

The top option is to turn the plugin off altogether. This is useful when you're testing.

The next level is **Simple** and the one you should try first. Select it and save the changes. Go and check your website. Has this fixed the mixed content issues you were unable to fix manually?

If so, that's it, job done. If not, then try the next level of fixing called **Content**. This is the one I usually end up with myself as it fixes the mixed content within my plugin code:

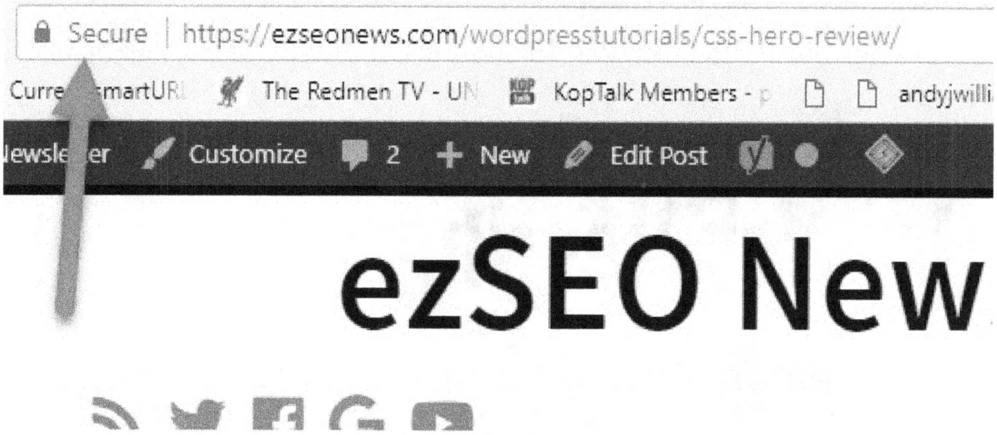

Secure
https://ezseonews.com/wordpresstutorials/css-hero-review/
The Redmen TV - UN
KopTalk Members -
andyjwilli
Customize
2
New
Edit Post
ezSEO New

My page now loads the padlock and **Secure** message.

The Insecure content extension in Chrome no longer reports any issues:

esstutorials/css-hero-review/
No Mixed Content Detected.
Locate

The **Content** level of fixing worked in this case. My site is now secure and returning the much-coveted padlock.

I want to show you one more thing before we leave this section. The plugin that was causing the issues was using resources accessed via insecure URLs. These resources were fonts. Because they were insecure, when my page loaded, the web browser blocked those fonts from downloading. Therefore, my browser used default fonts and gave the error message.

Here's how the banner looked with the browser default fonts before I fixed the mixed content issue:

40% Off Web Hosting
(the same host I personally use for all of my niche sites)
See why I use them...
Order Hosting
Use coupon Code: ezseonews

After installing the plugin, the fonts now load through a secure connection so we get the original fonts.

Notice how the banner fonts are different:

40% Off Web Hosting
(the same host I personally use for all of my niche sites)
See why I use them...
Order Hosting
Use coupon Code: ezseonews

OK, with everything working as intended, there are now a few housekeeping tasks we need to attend to.

A Little Housekeeping

1. Robots.txt File?

Do you use a robots.txt file on your website and include a link to the sitemap? If yes, make sure you update the link so that it points to your secure HTTPS sitemap.

2. Disavow Tool?

If you use Google's disavow tool on URLs that point to your HTTP site, re-upload the disavow file for your new HTTPS website.

3. Hard-Coded Links?

When you add links from one page of your site to another, there are good ways and bad ways of doing it.

The GOOD way is to use WordPress' built-in link tool to find the page you want to link to and link to it that way.

The BAD way is to hard code a link. In other words, inserting the exact URL that you want to link to.

When you write the body of your page or post, it's easy to stick with the built-in "good" method. However, there are places where this may not be possible.

For example:

1. When entering URLs into widgets.
2. When building custom menus.

The redirect we set up in the .htaccess file will actually deal with these. Even so, it's always better to fix at the source when you can.

4. Update Google Analytics

If you use Google Analytics to track your website, log in and choose the site you have just converted.

Next, click on the **Admin** link in the sidebar:

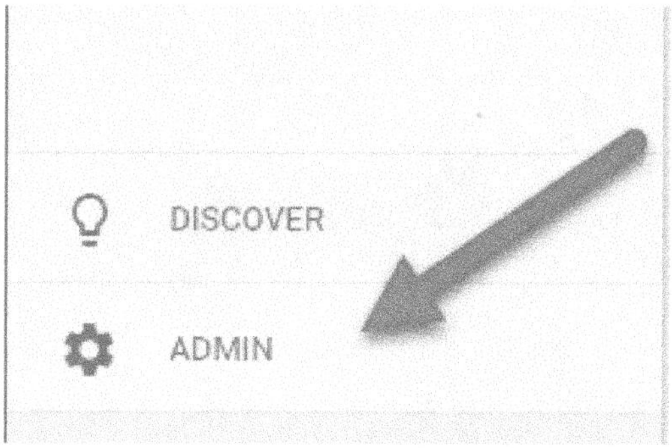
DISCOVER
ADMIN

Under **PROPERTY**, select **Property Settings**.

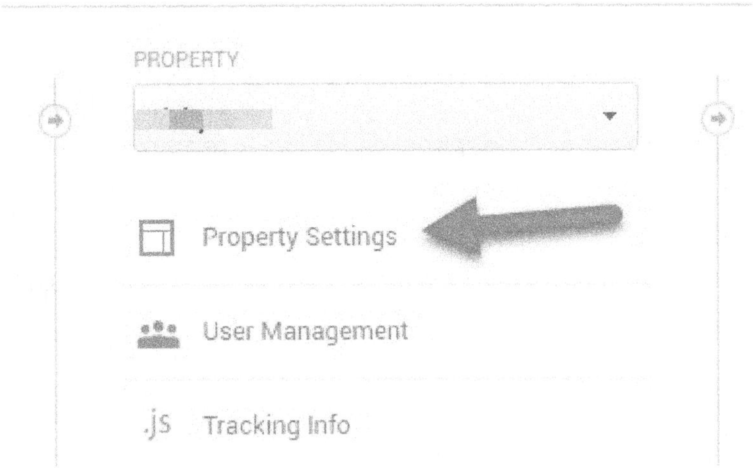
PROPERTY
Property Settings
User Management
.js Tracking Info

Then in the **Default URL**, choose **HTTPs://:**

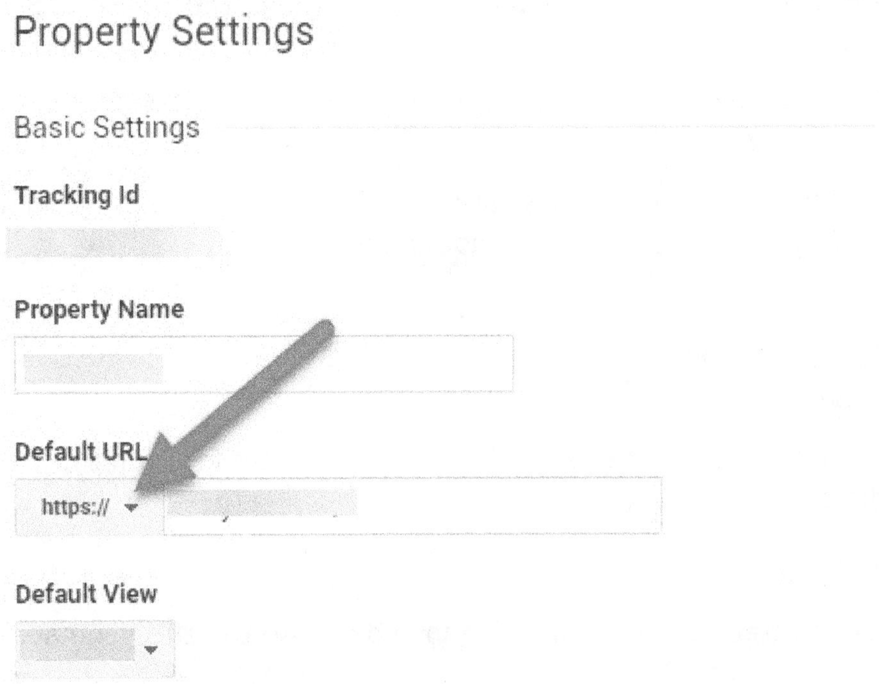
Property Settings
Basic Settings
Tracking Id
Property Name
Default URL
https://
Default View

Scroll to the bottom and click on the **Save** button.

Now click on the back button (top left):

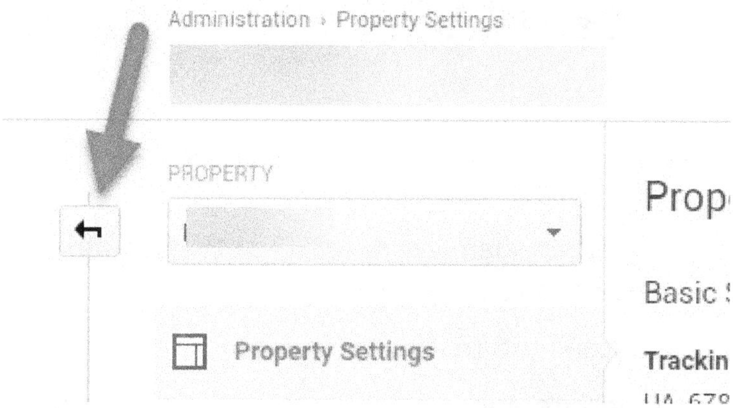
Administration › Property Settings
PROPERTY
Prop
Basic
Property Settings
Trackin

Under the **VIEW** section, click on **View Settings**.

VIEW
View Settings
User Management

You will find the **Website's URL** Within those settings which you need to change to **HTTPS.**

Save the page when you've done that.

5. Add to Search Console

If you use Google Search Console, you need to submit the HTTPS version of the site and verify it.

Once verified, remember to add your sitemap using the HTTPS version.

Unfortunately, you cannot submit a site move for a protocol change (HTTP to HTTPS) like you can when you move a site to a new domain. Therefore, you should keep both the HTTP and HTTPS versions in Search Console. This way lets you keep an eye on what is happening.

Over time, you'll find that pages indexed in the HTTP version will drop off while those in the HTTPS version increase. Once Google has completely deindexed the old HTTP version you can then delete it from Search Console.

SECTION 4 - Changing a Certificate e.g. AutoSSL to Encrypt It or Cloudflare

Maybe you started off with AutoSSL but now want to change to a different certificate? It's a fairly simple job which we'll cover in this chapter.

I have had to do this on a few of my own sites when the AutoSSL certificate did not renew properly. There are a few options open to you if you're in this situation:

1. If your host supports **Let's Encrypt SLL**, then use that.

2. Generate an **Origin Certificate** on **Cloudflare** and replace your existing certificate with that. Alternatively, you may have bought an SSL certificate that you want to use and that's fine too.

Let's look at both options.

Using Let's Encrypt

You can find more information about Let's Encrypt on their website:

HTTPs://letsencrypt.org/

Let's Encrypt certificates are free and automated but they also have to renew every few months. You may end up having problems with the auto-renewal as you did with the AutoSSL. Anyway, it's easy to setup (and change later if we want) so let's go ahead and do it.

The first step is to see whether your host supports Let's Encrypt. Login to cPanel and scroll down to the **SECURITY** section:

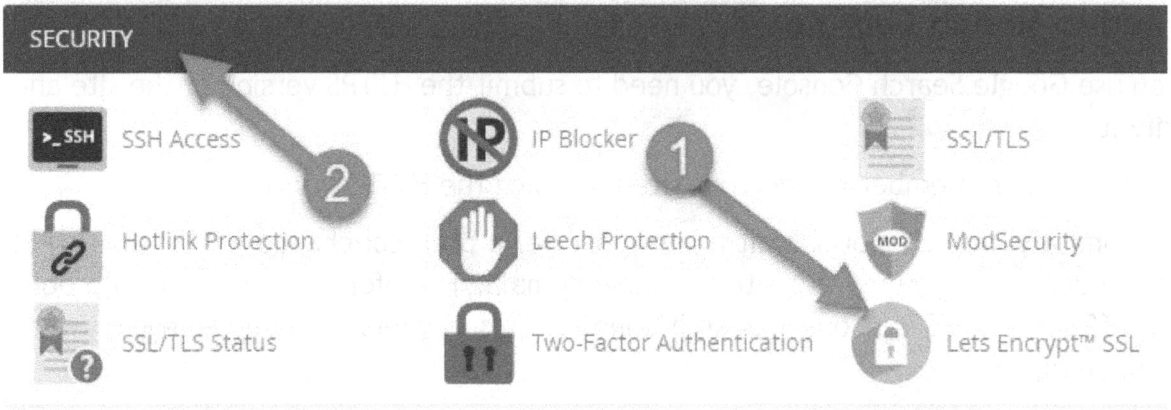
SECURITY
SSH Access
IP Blocker
SSL/TLS
Hotlink Protection
Leech Protection
ModSecurity
SSL/TLS Status
Two-Factor Authentication
Lets Encrypt™ SSL
1
2

Do you see the **Let's Encrypt SSL** icon? If you do, then happy days! The host I recommend fully supports this initiative which is another reason I recommend them.

Changing the AutoSSL certificate to Let's Encrypt is pretty easy.

Click on the **Let's Encrypt** icon in cPanel.

At the top of the screen, you'll see a list of all domains in your hosting package that currently use Let's Encrypt certificates. In your case, you probably don't have any yet.

Scroll down the page to find the **Issue a new certificate** section.

You will see all domains in your hosting package. Find the one that you want to change. Here's the domain I'll be switching over:

illumnii.com
illumnii.cheebles.com, illumnii.com, mail.illumnii.com, www.illumnii.cheebles.com, www.illumnii.com,
Issue

Here's the certificate currently in use by that domain before we do the switch:

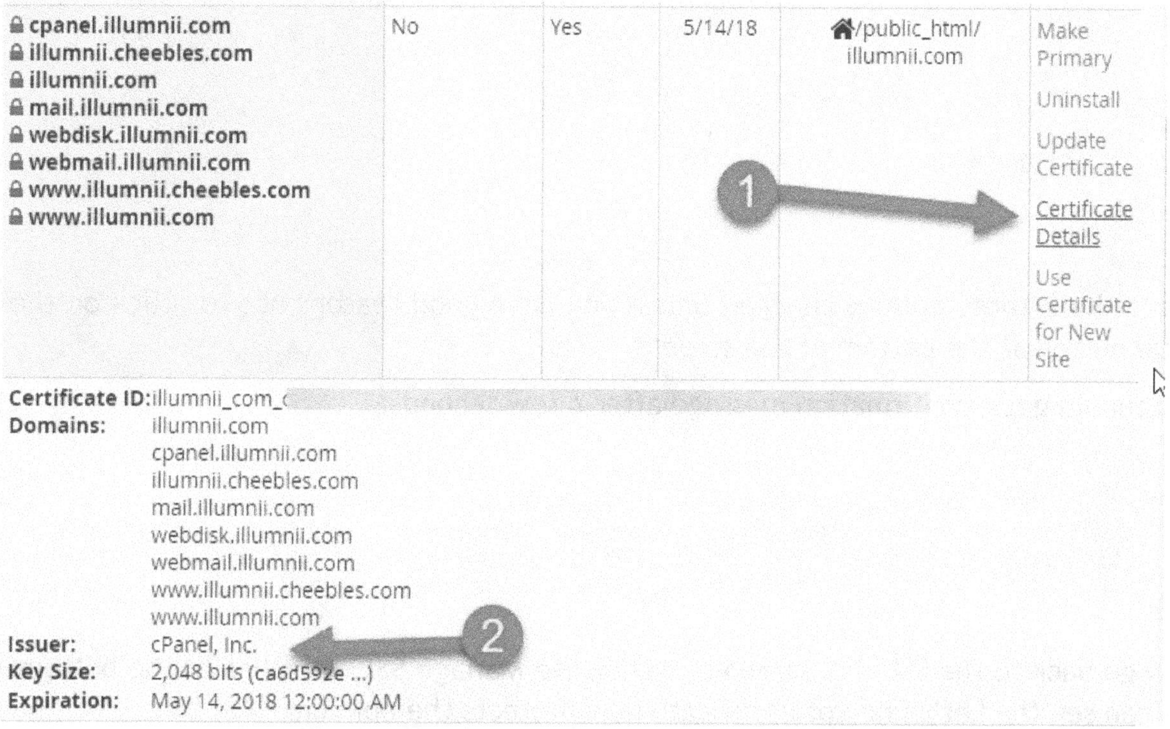
cpanel.illumnii.com
illumnii.cheebles.com
illumnii.com
mail.illumnii.com
webdisk.illumnii.com
webmail.illumnii.com
www.illumnii.cheebles.com
www.illumnii.com
No
Yes
5/14/18
/public_html/illumnii.com
Make Primary
Uninstall
Update Certificate
Certificate Details
Use Certificate for New Site
1
Certificate ID: illumnii_com_
Domains: illumnii.com
cpanel.illumnii.com
illumnii.cheebles.com
mail.illumnii.com
webdisk.illumnii.com
webmail.illumnii.com
www.illumnii.cheebles.com
www.illumnii.com
Issuer: cPanel, Inc.
Key Size: 2,048 bits (ca6d592e ...)
Expiration: May 14, 2018 12:00:00 AM
2

NOTE: You can find this information if you go to **SSL/TLS** in the **SECURITY** section of cPanel. You then choose **Install and Manage SSL for your site (HTTPS)**. Find your domain then click on the **Certificate Details** link.

You can see in my screenshot that cPanel (AutoSSL) issued the certificate.

OK, let's change that for the Let's Encrypt certificate.

Back on the Let's Encrypt screen, click on the **Issue** button next to your domain:

illumnii.com
illumnii.cheebles.com, illumnii.com,
mail.illumnii.com,
www.illumnii.cheebles.com,
www.illumnii.com,
Issue

You will see a screen that asks you what to include in the certificate. There's likely to be three boxes checked by default:

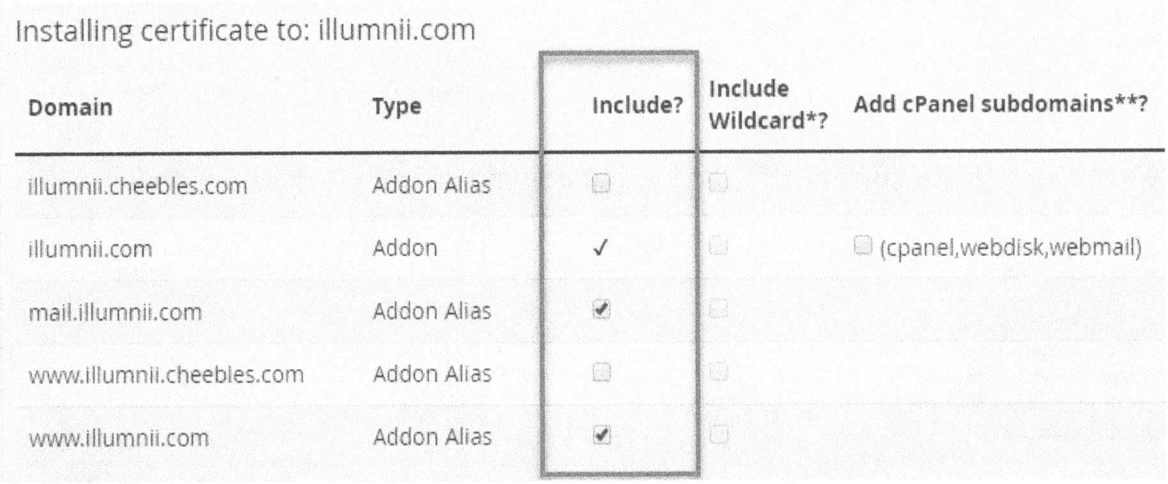
Installing certificate to: illumnii.com

Domain	Type	Include?	Include Wildcard*?	Add cPanel subdomains**?
illumnii.cheebles.com	Addon Alias	☐	☐	
illumnii.com	Addon	✓	☐	☐ (cpanel,webdisk,webmail)
mail.illumnii.com	Addon Alias	☑	☐	
www.illumnii.cheebles.com	Addon Alias	☐	☐	
www.illumnii.com	Addon Alias	☑	☐	

Leave those three options checked unless you have good reasons not to. Click on the **Issue** button at the bottom of the screen.

You should get a confirmation message after a few seconds:

The SSL certificate is now installed onto the domain "illumnii.com-alias of 'illumnii.cheebles.com'" using the IP address "184.154.46.243". The existing virtual host was updated with the new certificate. Apache is restarting in the background.

Now go back to the SSL/TLS screen and click the **Manage SSL Sites** link at the bottom. We can see the Let's Encrypt certificate now protects the domain:

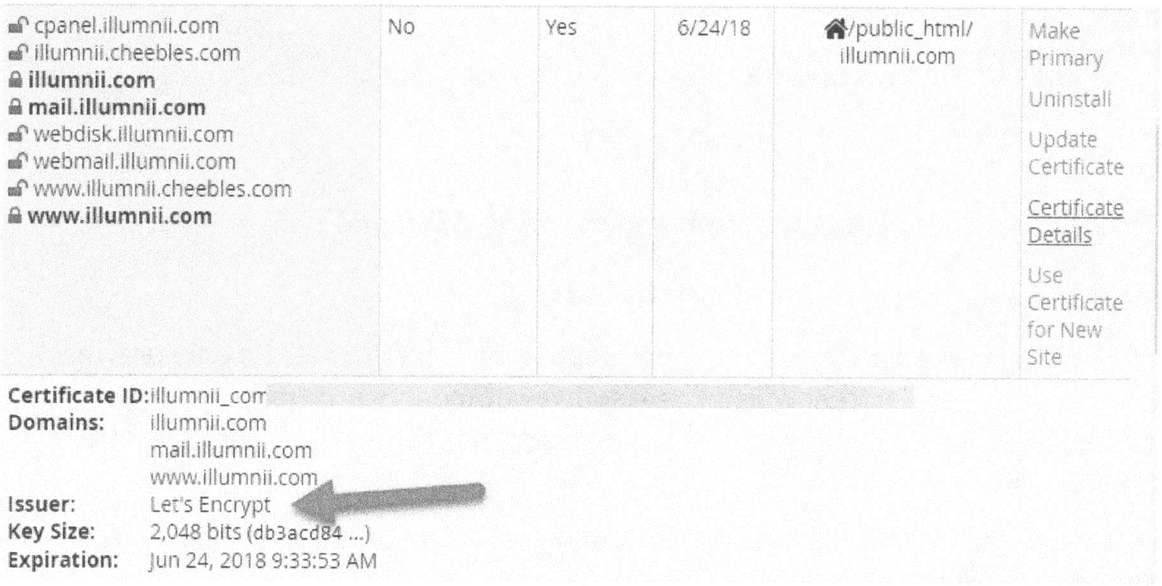
cpanel.illumnii.com
illumnii.cheebles.com
illumnii.com
mail.illumnii.com
webdisk.illumnii.com
webmail.illumnii.com
www.illumnii.cheebles.com
www.illumnii.com
No
Yes
6/24/18
/public_html/ illumnii.com
Make Primary
Uninstall
Update Certificate
Certificate Details
Use Certificate for New Site
Certificate ID:illumnii_
Domains: illumnii.com
mail.illumnii.com
www.illumnii.com
Issuer: Let's Encrypt
Key Size: 2,048 bits (db3acd84 ...)
Expiration: Jun 24, 2018 9:33:53 AM

If you want to delete the old certificates, you can. Just follow the instructions from earlier in this book in the section **Delete existing Origin Certificates for this Domain.** You can easily see which one(s) to delete:

illumnii.com
cpanel.illumnii.com
illumnii.cheebles.com
mail.illumnii.com
webdisk.illumnii.com
webmail.illumnii.com
www.illumnii.cheebles.com
www.illumnii.com
cPanel, Inc.
12/12/17
2048
Cert for "illumnii.cheebles.com"
Edit
Delete
Install
illumnii.com
mail.illumnii.com
www.illumnii.com
Let's Encrypt
6/24/18
2048
illumnii.com, mail.illumnii.com, and www.illumnii.com
Edit
Delete
Install

Make sure you keep the **Let's Encrypt** certificate and just delete those issued by cPanel. The AutoSSL should disable when you delete the old certificates so it doesn't attempt to renew them. This is the way my recommended host works. If you use a different host get familiar with it first if things are slightly different.

OK, we're done here. You've changed your old certificate to a Let's Encrypt certificate. If you ever want to remove the Let's Encrypt certificate it's also a simple process. Just go into the Let's Encrypt section of cPanel and find your domain in the list at the top of the page:

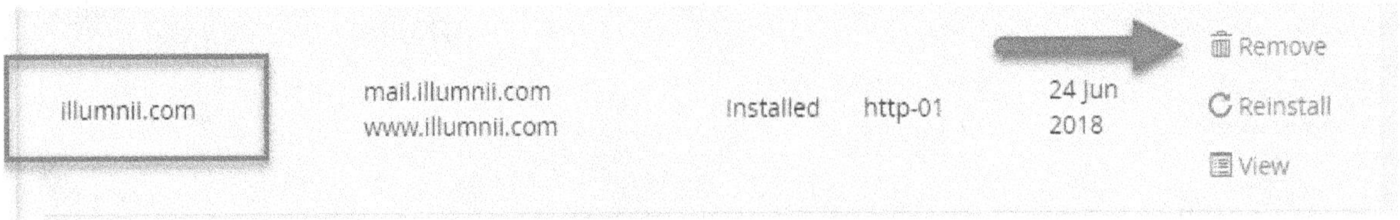
illumnii.com
mail.illumnii.com
www.illumnii.com
Installed
http-01
24 Jun
2018
Remove
Reinstall
View

To remove the certificate, click the **Remove** link on the right.

Swap for Cloudflare Origin Certificate

Let's Encrypt is becoming more and more popular as a certificate. Its only drawback is that it requires regular renewing. There's always Cloudflare if you decide you don't want the hassle of checking whether a certificate has renewed. Cloudflare offers 15-year certificates.

Let's switch the certificate we just installed for a Cloudflare certificate. Your site should already be in Cloudflare.

If it isn't, add it now. In your domain registrar, make sure your domain's DNS is set to the Cloudflare DNS you're given.

OK, login to Cloudflare and click on the **Crypto** tab at the top:

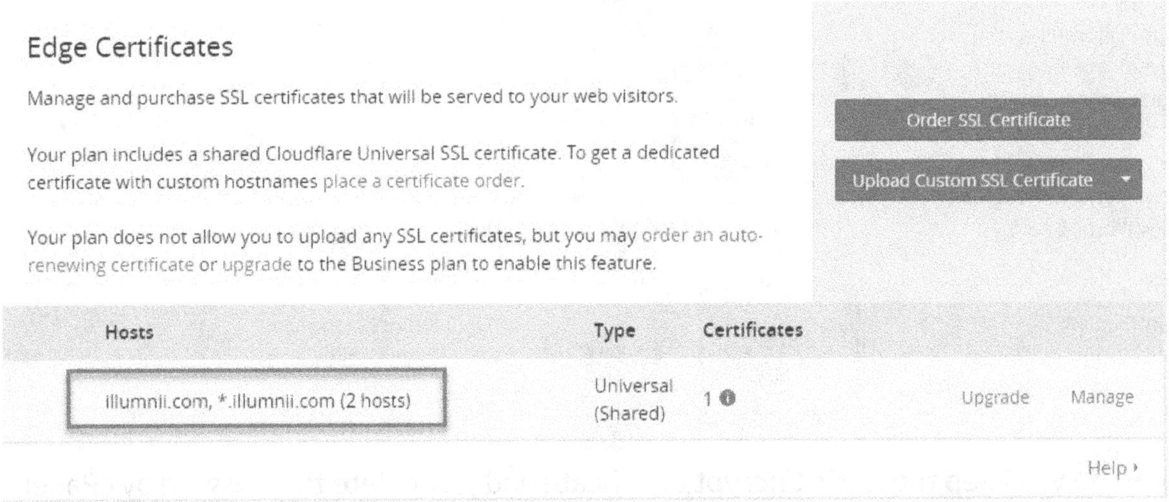
Edge Certificates
Manage and purchase SSL certificates that will be served to your web visitors.
Your plan includes a shared Cloudflare Universal SSL certificate. To get a dedicated certificate with custom hostnames place a certificate order.
Your plan does not allow you to upload any SSL certificates, but you may order an auto-renewing certificate or upgrade to the Business plan to enable this feature.
Order SSL Certificate
Upload Custom SSL Certificate
Hosts
Type
Certificates
illumnii.com, *.illumnii.com (2 hosts)
Universal (Shared)
1
Upgrade
Manage
Help

Your site should have **Edge certificates** issued by Cloudflare. If it doesn't, you'll need to go back in the book to make sure your site's added and the DNS is updated.

Your site won't have an origin certificate as we've not created one yet.

Let's create it now.

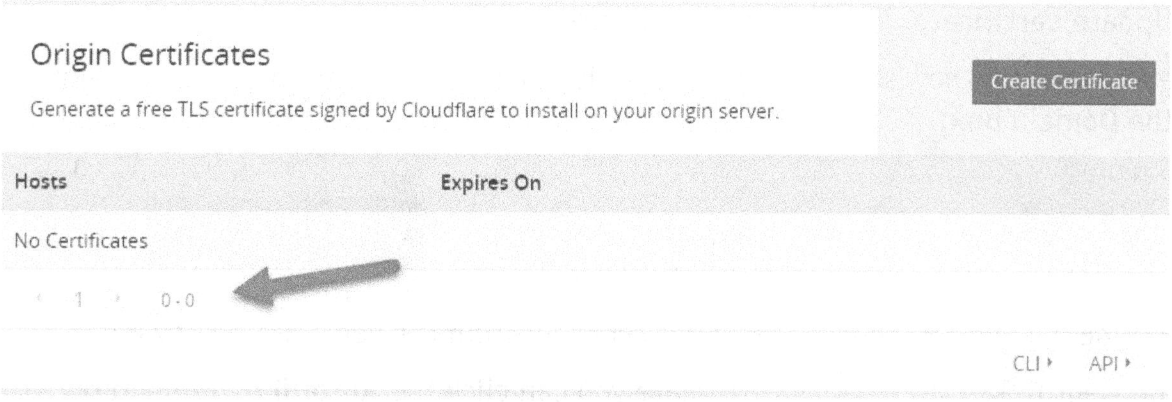
Origin Certificates
Generate a free TLS certificate signed by Cloudflare to install on your origin server.
Create Certificate
Hosts
Expires On
No Certificates
1
0 - 0
CLI
API

This is the same process we saw earlier in the book.

Click on the **Create Certificate** button in the **Origin Certificates** section.

Leave all the settings at their default on the **Origin Certificate** Installation screen and click **Next.**

The certificate and primary key will display on the screen. Do not close this screen.

To install the certificate we have the following two options:

1. Uninstall the previous Let's Encrypt certificate and then install this one.
2. Simply replace the existing certificate with the new origin certificate.

This site is currently set to Full (strict) on the Crypto tab In Cloudflare. Remember that Full (strict) means two certificates are needed; an Edge certificate and an origin certificate. If we uninstall the current certificate, the HTTPS version of our site will be unavailable until the new one is in place.

This is why I recommend you replace the existing certificate with the new one.

In cPanel, click on **SSL/TLS** in the **SECURITY** section. Then click on **Manage SSL sites** at the bottom.

Scroll down until you find your website:

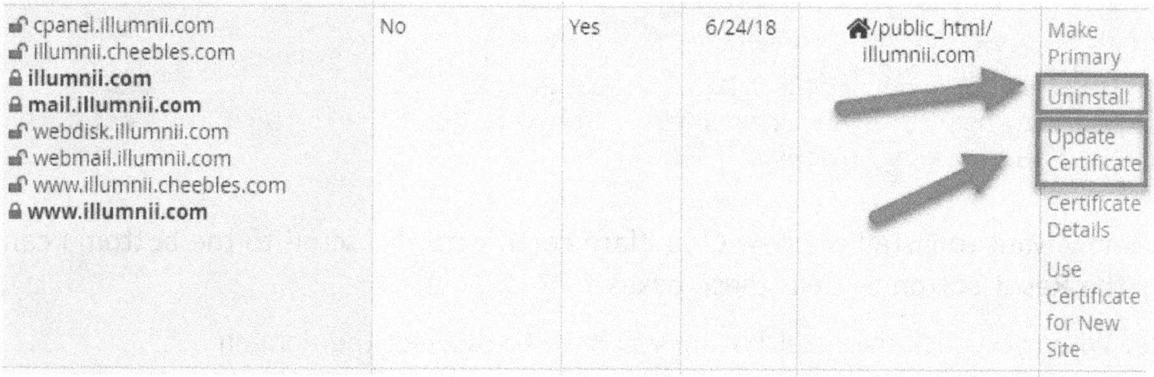
cpanel.illumnii.com
illumnii.cheebles.com
illumnii.com
mail.illumnii.com
webdisk.illumnii.com
webmail.illumnii.com
www.illumnii.cheebles.com
www.illumnii.com
No
Yes
6/24/18
/public_html/ illumnii.com
Make Primary
Uninstall
Update Certificate
Certificate Details
Use Certificate for New Site

In the column on the right, you can see the option to **uninstall** the current certificate or **Update certificate**. Click on **Update Certificate**.

The screen should now scroll to the bottom with your domain name automatically added to the **Domain box:**

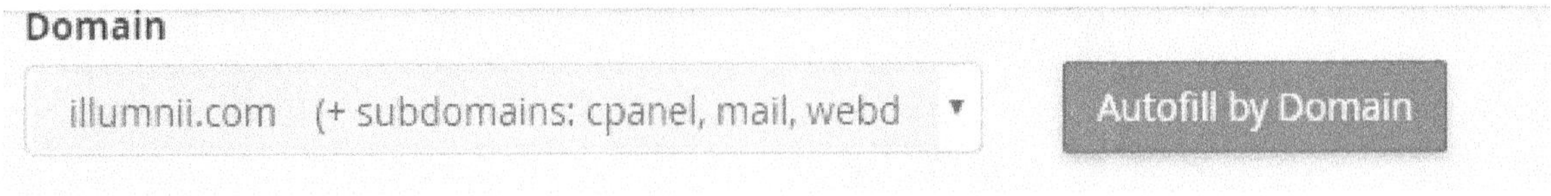
Domain
illumnii.com (+ subdomains: cpanel, mail, webd
Autofill by Domain

If your domain doesn't display correctly, choose it from the domain drop down box.

If you want to see the existing certificate you can click the **Autofill by Domain** button and the current certificate will load. You can see that mine is the Let's Encrypt certificate we installed earlier in the chapter.

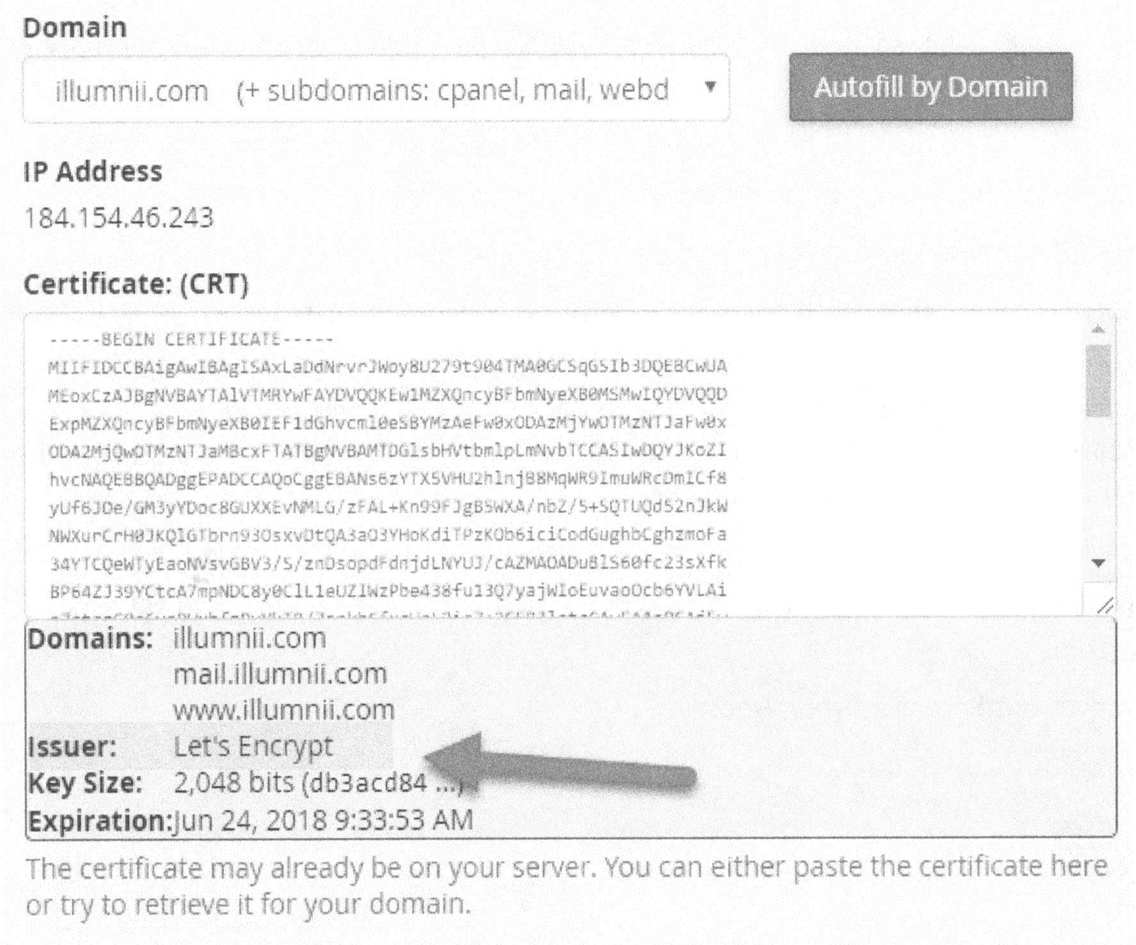
Domain
illumnii.com (+ subdomains: cpanel, mail, webd
Autofill by Domain
IP Address
184.154.46.243
Certificate: (CRT)
-----BEGIN CERTIFICATE-----
Domains: illumnii.com
mail.illumnii.com
www.illumnii.com
Issuer: Let's Encrypt
Key Size: 2,048 bits (db3acd84 ...)
Expiration: Jun 24, 2018 9:33:53 AM
The certificate may already be on your server. You can either paste the certificate here or try to retrieve it for your domain.

OK, I now want to install the new Cloudflare certificate. If I scroll to the bottom I can click the **Reset** button to clear these boxes.

Note: When you click the reset button you have to reselect the domain.

It's now a case of copying and pasting the **Certificate** and **Private Key** from Cloudflare, into these boxes.

First, select the entire **Origin Certificate**, including -----BEGIN CERTIFICATE----- and -----END CERTIFICATE-----:

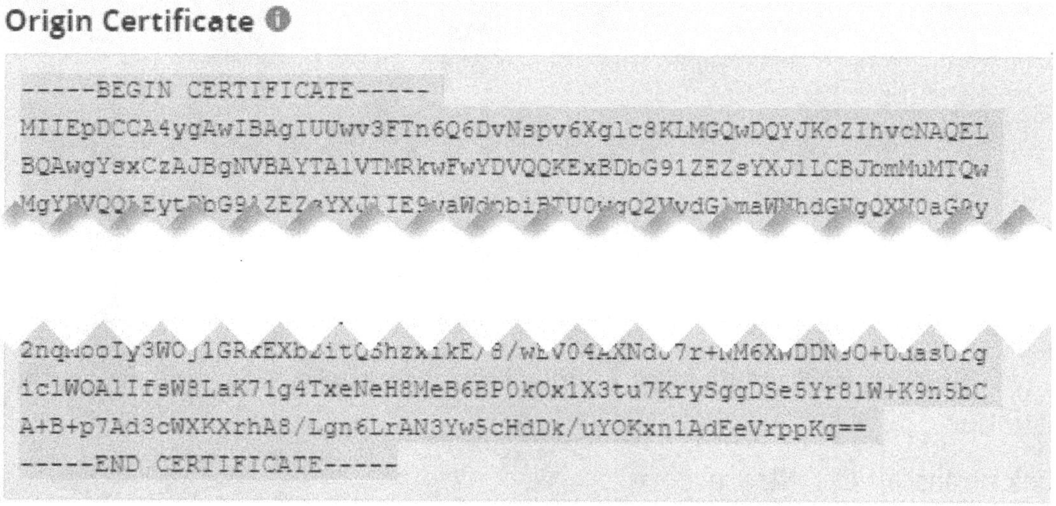
Origin Certificate
-----BEGIN CERTIFICATE-----
MIIEpDCCA4ygAwIBAgIUUwv3FTn6Q6DvNspv6Xglc8KLMGQwDQYJKoZIhvcNAQEL
BQAwgYsxCzAJBgNVBAYTAlVTMRkwFwYDVQQKExBDbG91ZEZsYXJlLCBJbmMuMTQw
iclWOAlIfsW8LaK71g4TxeNeH8MeB6BP0kOx1X3tu7KrySggDSe5Yr81W+K9n5bC
A+B+p7Ad3cWXKXrhA8/Lgn6LrAN3Yw5cHdDk/uYOKxn1AdEeVrppKg==
-----END CERTIFICATE-----

Paste that data into the **Certificate: (CRT)** box in cPanel:

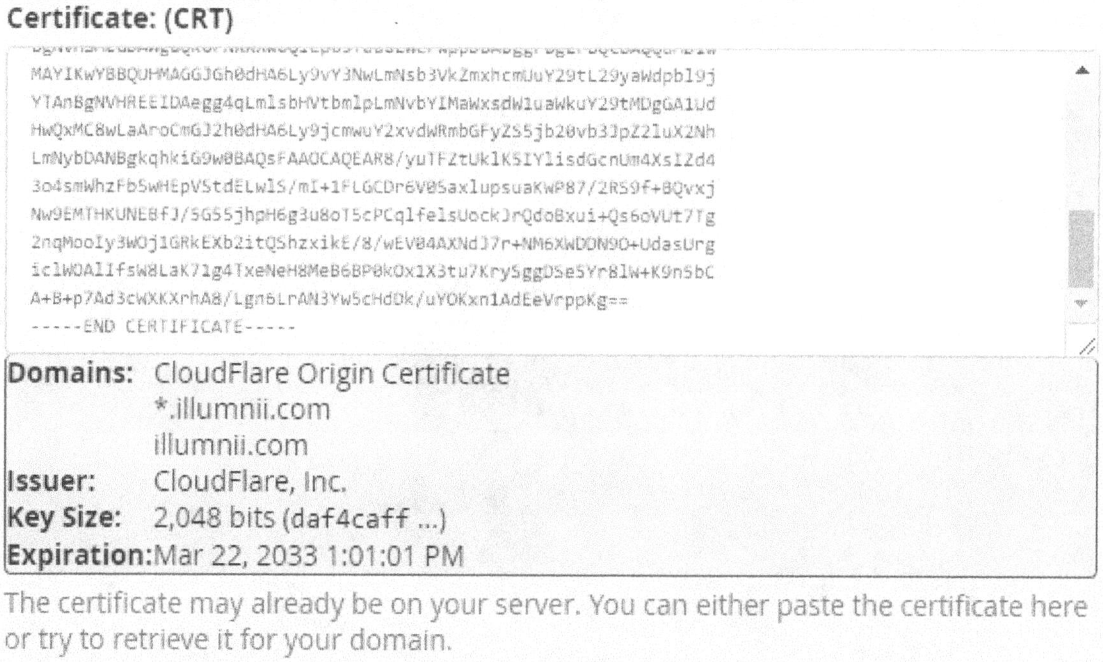
Certificate: (CRT)
-----END CERTIFICATE-----
Domains: CloudFlare Origin Certificate
*.illumnii.com
illumnii.com
Issuer: CloudFlare, Inc.
Key Size: 2,048 bits (daf4caff ...)
Expiration: Mar 22, 2033 1:01:01 PM
The certificate may already be on your server. You can either paste the certificate here or try to retrieve it for your domain.

Repeat the process for the **Private Key** and paste its data into the box in cPanel:

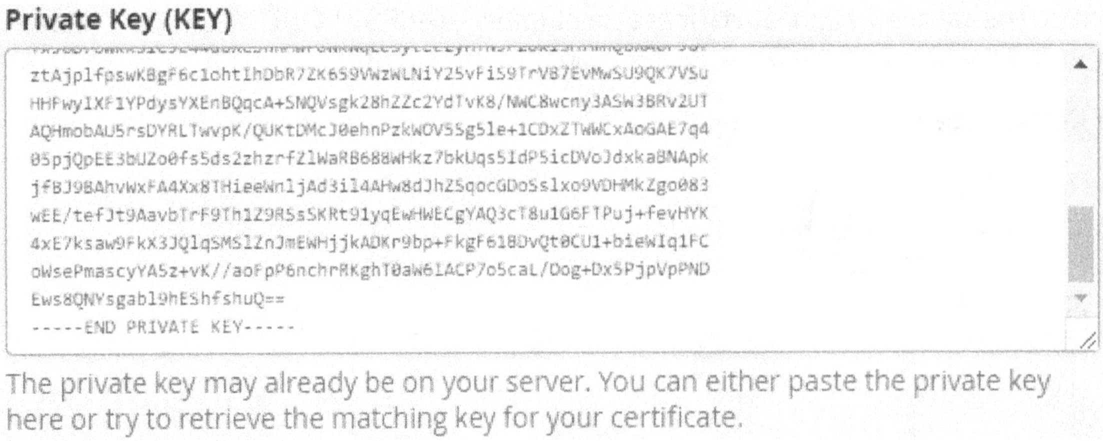
Private Key (KEY)
ztAjplfpswK8gF6clohtIhDbR7ZK659VWzWLNiY25vFi59TrVB7EvMwSU9QK7VSu
HHFwylXF1YPdysYXEnBQqcA+SNQVsgk28hZZc2YdTvK8/NWC8wcny3ASW3BRv2UT
AQHmobAU5rsDYRLTwvpK/QUKtDMcJ0ehnPzkWOV55g5le+1CDxZTWWCxAoGAE7q4
05pjQpEE3bUZo0fs5ds2zhzrfZlWaRB688WHkz7bkUqs5IdP5icDVoJdxkaBNApk
jfBJ9BAhvWxFA4Xx8THieeWnljAd3il4AHw8dJh25qocGDoSslxo9VDHMkZgo083
wEE/tefJt9AavbTrF9Th1Z9R5sSKRt91yqEwHWECgYAQ3cT8u1G6FTPuj+fevHYK
4xE7ksaw9FkX3JQ1qSMSlZnJmEWHjjkADKr9bp+FkgF618DvQt0CU1+bieWIq1FC
oWsePmascyYA5z+vK//aoFpP6nchrRKghT0aW6lACP7o5caL/Dog+Dx5PjpVpPND
Ews8QNYsgabl9hEShfshuQ==
-----END PRIVATE KEY-----
The private key may already be on your server. You can either paste the private key here or try to retrieve the matching key for your certificate.

You can leave the Certificate Authority Bundle empty as the system will fetch that during installation.

OK, now click on **Install Certificate.**

If all goes well, you'll see a message to say the installation was successful.

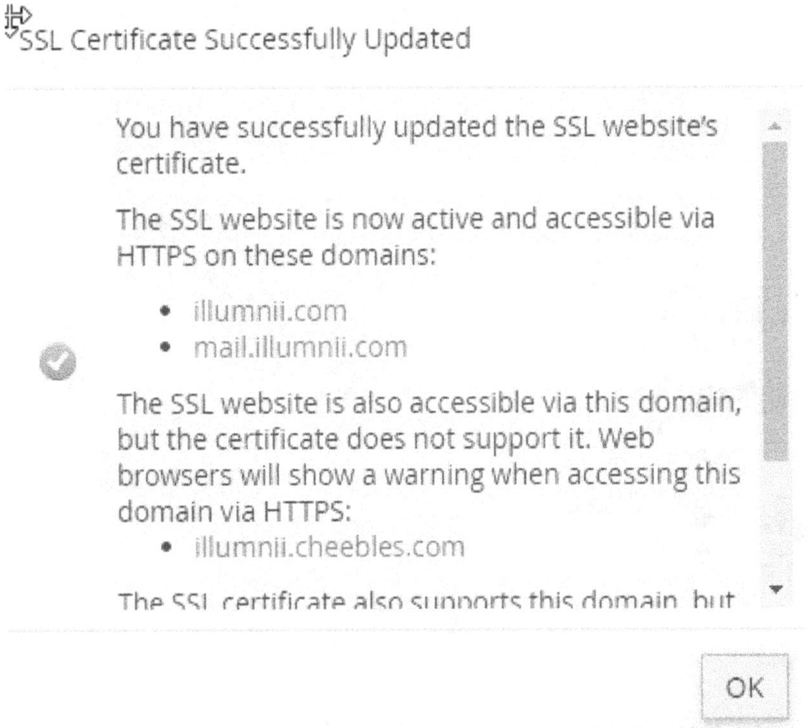
SSL Certificate Successfully Updated
You have successfully updated the SSL website's certificate.
The SSL website is now active and accessible via HTTPS on these domains:
illumnii.com
mail.illumnii.com
The SSL website is also accessible via this domain, but the certificate does not support it. Web browsers will show a warning when accessing this domain via HTTPS:
illumnii.cheebles.com
OK

Find your site again in the list on the Manage SSL Hosts screen. It should confirm the correct installation of your new certificate:

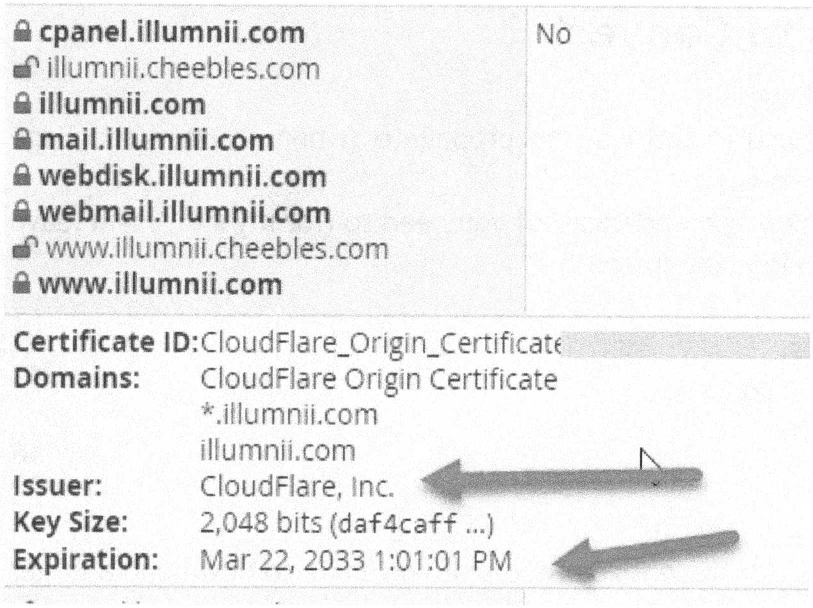
cpanel.illumnii.com
illumnii.cheebles.com
illumnii.com
mail.illumnii.com
webdisk.illumnii.com
webmail.illumnii.com
www.illumnii.cheebles.com
www.illumnii.com
No
Certificate ID:CloudFlare_Origin_Certificate
Domains:
CloudFlare Origin Certificate
*.illumnii.com
illumnii.com
Issuer:
CloudFlare, Inc.
Key Size:
2,048 bits (daf4caff ...)
Expiration:
Mar 22, 2033 1:01:01 PM

As you can see, CloudFlare, Inc. is now the issuer for the certificate on this site. The certificate expires on March 22, 2033 (15 years from now).

If you're moving away from Let's Encrypt, go to the Let's Encrypt page of cPanel.

illumnii.com
mail.illumnii.com
www.illumnii.com
Not installed
http-01
24 Jun 2018
Remove
Reinstall
View

The old certificate is 'not installed' but it's still there. I recommend you click the **Remove** link to delete the Let's Encrypt certificate for this site.

The last thing to do is visit your site. It should load using HTTPs.

NOTE: You may need to clear the cache in your browser. If your site doesn't load for any reason, check the origin and edge certificates are both installed correctly.

Appendix – Steps to Convert

1. Add the Site to Cloudflare.
2. Change DNS at the registrar and wait to propagate (when you see the Edge Certificate you can move on).
3. Generate and install the origin certificate if you need to (for my site, I will leave the AutoSSL certificate in place instead).
4. Secure the Dashboard.
5. HTACCESS file redirects.
6. Check SSL and fix mixed content.
7. Insecure content plugin.
8. Google Analytics.
9. Search Console.

On the next page is a flowchart of the entire process. If you'd like to download a larger PDF copy you can do that via this link:

https://ezseonews.com/httpsflow/

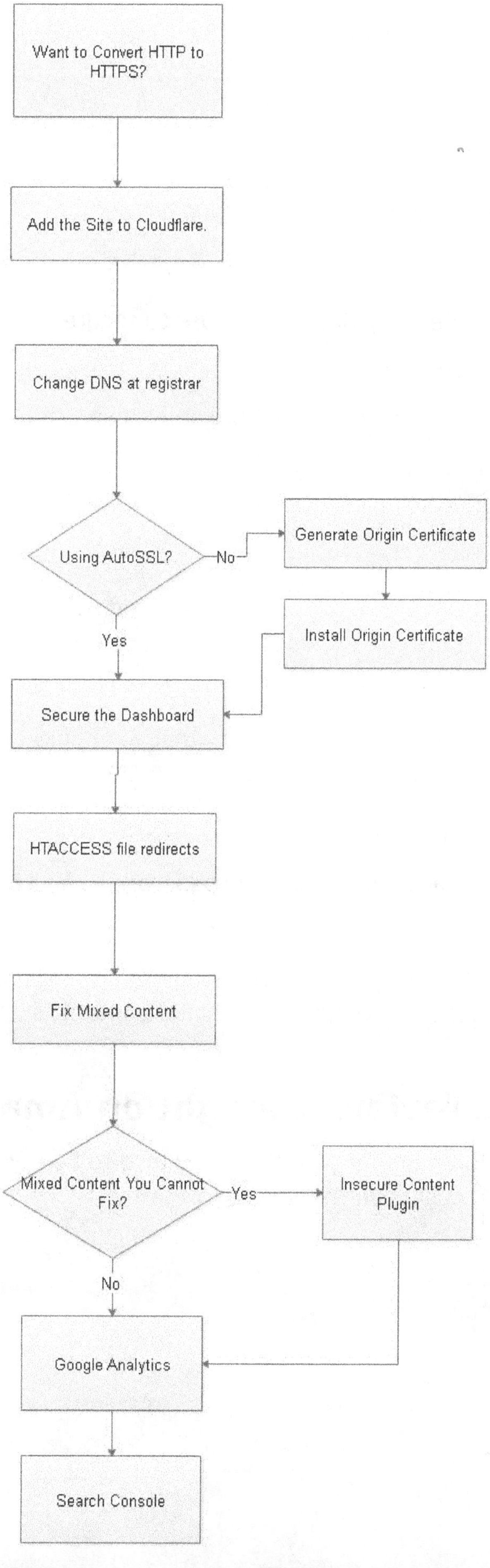

Want to Convert HTTP to HTTPS?
Add the Site to Cloudflare.
Change DNS at registrar
Using AutoSSL?
No
Generate Origin Certificate
Install Origin Certificate
Yes
Secure the Dashboard
HTACCESS file redirects
Fix Mixed Content
Mixed Content You Cannot Fix?
Yes
Insecure Content Plugin
No
Google Analytics
Search Console

Where to go from here?

Congratulations! We've covered a lot of ground in this book but you should now be confident converting your HTTP site to HTTPS.

But what if you still have questions?

Below is a list of useful resources to help you find answers.

Relevant Web Sites

Cloudflare - The Content Delivery Network we use to secure the site:

https://www.cloudflare.com/

SSL Insecure Content Fixer - The WordPress plugin we can use to fix "unfixable" mixed content:

https://en-gb.wordpress.org/plugins/ssl-insecure-content-fixer/

My Video Courses

I have a growing number of video courses hosted on Udemy, including a complimentary course on converting a site to HTTPS. You can view a complete list of these at my site:

https://ezseonews.com/udemy

There are courses on the same kinds of topics that my books cover, so SEO, Content Creation, WordPress, Website Analytics, etc.

My other Webmaster books

All my books are available as Kindle books and paperbacks. You can view them all here:

https://amazon.com/author/drandrewwilliams

I'll leave you to explore those if you are interested. You'll find books on various aspects of being a webmaster, such as creating high-quality content, SEO, CSS etc.

Please leave a review/thought on Amazon

If you enjoyed this book, or even if you didn't, I'd love to hear your comments about it. You can leave your thoughts on the Amazon website.

www.ingramcontent.com/pod-product-compliance
Lightning Source LLC
Chambersburg PA
CBHW080559060326
40689CB00021B/4894